THINKING CRITICALLY
ABOUT CRITICAL
THINKING

THINKING CRITICALLY ABOUT CRITICAL THINKING

Diane F. Halpern
California State University
San Bernardino

LAWRENCE ERLBAUM ASSOCIATES, PUBLISHERS

1996   Mahwah, New Jersey

Lawrence Erlbaum Associates, Inc., Publishers
10 Industrial Avenue
Mahwah, New Jersey 07430

Cover design by Robert Perine

Books published by Lawrence Erlbaum Associates are printed on acid-free paper, and their bindings are chosen for strength and durability.

Printed in the United States of America
10 9 8 7 6 5 4 3 2

CONTENTS

TO THE READER

Thinking is not a spectator sport. Research has shown that the skills of critical thinking must be practiced with a wide variety of problems in many different contexts in order to be learned and retained. The exercises, questions, and reviews in this exercise book are designed to provide the systematic practice that is needed to help you become a more critical thinker. Every chapter begins with 10 true–false questions that you should answer *before* you read the accompanying chapter in the text *Thought and Knowledge: An Introduction to Critical Thinking* (3rd ed.). By reading and responding to the questions before you read, you will be developing a framework that will help you to comprehend, anticipate, and organize the information in the accompanying chapter. It is a good way to prepare for reading.

The true–false questions are followed by a brief statement of the chapter objectives. Read this short section carefully because it will help you to anticipate the reason for the chapter and what I want you, the reader, to get out of it. Two pages are then reserved for your journal entries. This is a very open exercise in which you can be analytic, creative, or even critical. This is a place to reflect on your learning, judge how well it is going, and relate new material to other topics. Students often find that they gain insights into what they know by setting aside two separate times to write about each chapter. Sometimes these journals are wonderfully creative, and almost always they are useful tools for learning and thinking. A list of skills is then presented in a matrix. The skills matrix serves as a brief reminder and review so that you can quickly go over the thinking skills that were presented in each chapter. The most interesting and challenging of the exercises involves applying the skills to a variety of different contexts. This active learning component makes it more likely that you will remember to use what you are learning when you need the skills in real-world settings. In the jargon of cognitive psychology, it promotes transfer of learning. Finally, a series of thoughtful questions is posed to serve as a check on your understanding and recall of the material in each chapter.

All of the exercises were written to be similar to problems and situations that you are likely to encounter in your real life outside of class. Problems include topics like saving money, understanding a research report that appears in a newspaper, recognizing propaganda, reaching reasoned conclusions, avoiding common biases, and deciding when a risk is too risky. I hope that you will work through all of the exercises and that you will not only learn from them, but also enjoy at least some of them. Be sure to discuss interesting and puzzling ideas with others in your life. Another good way to be a good learner is to become a good teacher—both roles require a deep understanding of the issues and clarity about the concepts. Although I cannot promise that regular use of this exercise book will result in "brains of steel," it can make you a better thinker. Enjoy!

1

THINKING: AN INTRODUCTION

BEFORE YOU READ THE FIRST CHAPTER:
TRUE OR FALSE?

Circle the correct answer.

1. Americans routinely score higher than comparable test takers from other countries in international comparisons of academic and thinking skills.

        T   F

2. The use of critical thinking skills does NOT guarantee that you will always have a desirable outcome.

        T   F

3. Research has shown that people can learn in their sleep and can improve their ability to think with the use of appropriate subliminal messages that are placed on audiotapes.

        T   F

4. Biological studies of the brain have provided several useful suggestions for enhancing thinking skills.

        T   F

5. Most people report that they use images when they think.

        T   F

6. Intelligence can best be thought of as a fixed quantity that does not change over the lifetime.

        T   F

7. Most media depictions of people who think well are negative.

        T   F

8. A critical thinking attitude includes questioning every statement and using critical thinking skills in every situation.

T	F

9. People who have good metacognitive skills pay attention to what they are doing when they are thinking.

T	F

10. An advantage of a skills approach to critical thinking is that it allows a large body of material to be considered in smaller and more manageable units.

T	F

CHAPTER OBJECTIVES

The purpose of the first chapter is to provide a foundation for the topics that are discussed throughout the text. Arguments are made to convince the reader of the need to think critically in our increasingly complex world. Different ways of thinking about thinking are presented along with several conceptualizations of intelligence. It is clear that the attitude or disposition to think critically must be cultivated and valued. The purpose of the first chapter is to get the reader to think about thinking. Evidence is presented to support the conclusion that better thinking can result from courses designed for that purpose.

ACTIVE LEARNING EXERCISES

Writing as an Aid for Thinking

Because critical thinking is a skill that must be practiced if it is to be learned in a way that will promote transfer, there are several exercises presented for each chapter. All of the exercises are designed to involve the reader deeply and actively in concrete, useful experiences in critical thinking. One way to improve thinking skills is with writing. When people write, they are required to organize thoughts, make decisions about what is relevant and what is not, select the words that convey their thoughts, and arrive at a conclusion. Numerous psychologists have noted the close link between thinking and writing (e.g., McGovern & Hogshead, 1990; Wade, 1995). Writing is an important skill that is needed in every profession, and the only way to "get good at it" is to practice often.

1.1. Topic Analysis

Although the thinking skills are grouped and presented in many chapters, in fact there is a great deal of overlap among them. Most complex issues will require the use of many of the skills that are covered in the text. Here is a list of controversial, contemporary topics. Select one of them to work on throughout the term. Although the sort of information that is available for each topic will differ, almost all of them will require the use of evidence, understanding cause, solving problems, using language to persuade, and the other skills that are presented in later chapters.

As you work through the text, use the skills gained in each chapter to help formulate your conclusions about the topic you select. Be sure that the topic you select is one that you honestly don't have a strong opinion about at this time. This is important because research has shown that you will probably attend to information that confirms your beliefs and down-play the importance of information that is counter to your beliefs.

1. *Violence on television:* Does it have negative or positive effects? Does it desensitize children to violence? Does it serve as a socially acceptable way to relieve anger and hostility? Should the amount and type of violence that can be shown on television or other places be regulated in some way? Why?

2. *Needles to addicts:* One major concern with the spread of AIDS is the use of dirty needles by intravenous drug users. Should addicts be given clean needles to prevent the spread of AIDS? Will there be more addicts if the government supplies needles? Would the act of providing clean needles to addicts send the message that illegal drug use is OK? What is the evidence in support of your position?

3. *Capital punishment:* Does capital punishment deter crime? Is it cruel and unusual? What is cruel and unusual punishment? Does the definition of what is cruel and unusual depend on the time and culture, or is there a universal definition that is always true?

4. *Legalization of drugs:* One suggested solution to the drug problem is to make drug use legal, much like the way we have legalized alcohol consumption. Some think that it would eliminate virtually all drug-related crime and help addicts get the help they need. Others believe that it will encourage drug use and increase the number of addicts. Be sure to support your conclusion.

5. *Euthanasia:* Should euthanasia, the right to terminate one's own life, be decriminalized in this country? Would this action lead to many abuses and the death of many people who might have had happy lives? Is it ever justified? Who should decide?

6. *Parental rights:* Do parents have the right to know if their teenage-minor children (ages 13–17) purchase contraceptives, elect to have an abortion, or have a sexually transmitted disease? Parents have financial, legal, and moral responsibilities toward their children. What are the rights of parents when the information concerns their children's behavior and health?

7. *Day care:* Should the United States adopt a national policy on day care? Would this pose a serious risk to the traditional family and encourage parents to leave their young children with strangers for much of the day? Is quality day care a right like the right to a public education, or is it a costly luxury that will contribute to the breakup of families?

8. *Pornography:* Should pornography (involving either children or adults) be regulated in any way? Is this a violation of free speech? Is pornography harmful? How do you know? How can we define pornography?

9. *Pregnant women and drugs:* Should pregnant women who drink alcohol excessively or take illegal drugs be subjected to prosecution for putting their children at risk? Is this child abuse? Would it ultimately harm the children that such a law would be designed to protect?

10. *Teens and welfare:* A national columnist recently suggested that teenage mothers should not be given welfare payments so as to encourage them to work and get support from the father. Would this help or hurt society in general, the mothers, or their children? Is it a good idea?

When working on your topic analysis, you will have to consider what information you will need to support a conclusion. You will need to use most of the skills developed in the text as you work through your topic—how well your evidence supports your conclusion, the structure of the argument you are making, the use of empirical data, and identification of fallacious reasoning. Be sure to state a conclusion and provide good support for it. I hope that you will enjoy researching and thinking about the controversial topic you selected.

Guidelines for Topic Analysis Papers. This is an outline of some of the basic steps in writing your topic analysis paper. It is a useful guide that should be helpful with any writing assignment.

1. Consider your topic. What are the issues and arguments on both sides? Are there more than two sides? Does the nature of the conclusion depend on other variables such as the age of the participants or their income or intent? Be sure that you understand the issues. Discuss them with other interested people.

2. Start by researching the issue in the library and by examining the thinking behind each of the claims. Pay particular attention to the thinking skills that are presented in the text. Examine what others have said and thought about the topic. Consider the following:

   a. Empirical data—sample size, measurement, representativeness of the sample, possible bias in the data.
   b. Overgeneralization and the need for additional evidence.
   c. Definitions of terms and descriptions of issues.
   d. Flaws in statistical thinking.
   e. Failure to consider alternative options or solutions.
   f. Oversimplification of complex issues.
   g. Fallacies in thinking such as those listed in your text.
   h. Strength and relevance of reasons for different conclusions.
   i. Stated and unstated assumptions and counterarguments.
   j. Failure to seek disconfirming evidence.
   k. Misuse of language (e.g., vagueness, ambiguity, etc.).
   l. Belief and value biases.
   m. Analogies and emotional language.
   n. Other skills listed in each chapter. Go through them and see which other ones might apply to your topic.

3. Determine the basic points you want to make in your paper. What do you want readers to remember? Think about why you chose the topic and why it is important.

4. Make an outline or graphic organizer *before* you write. This should include:

a. Introduction—State the basic points that you want to make in your paper and the steps you will follow to make these points.

b. Description of the issues.

c. Analysis—Arguments, reasoning, evidence, data, expert opinions, analogies, etc. This is where you demonstrate your good thinking skills.

d. Conclusion—Succinctly restate your basic point (i.e., what the paper showed). Explain your ideas about the topic.

5. Go through your notes again to see if you should add or delete anything. Do you have further information that would be helpful in understanding your topic?

6. Revise your outline or graphic organizer as needed. Make sure that the ideas follow each other logically and support your conclusion. Is there anything in your outline that is not relevant to your topic? If so, delete it.

7. Write the first draft. If at all possible, learn and use a word processor. These are available in many places on college campuses and in private businesses where they can be rented by the hour. Many libraries also have word processors that can be used by the public. (If you plan to use a word processor, be sure to allow extra time for computer "glitches" such as "down" time and printers that will not cooperate.)

8. Check this draft for the following:

a. Writing style—Spelling, grammar, sentence structure, tone.

b. Content—Organization of the paper and logical development of ideas. Look over the entire paper and decide if anything is omitted that would clarify the points being made, if the order of the topics should be altered, or if the conclusion is well supported.

9. Revise the paper.

10. Check margins (usually 1" to 1½" all the way around), length (approximately five to eight pages, at a minimum, is needed to present some of the issues that relate to these topics—you may be asked to write a longer paper), double spacing, and completeness of title page information. Be sure that you reference all sources that you used. Review your college or university policy on plagiarism and honesty, if you are not familiar with it. Plagiarism, even if unintentional, is a serious offense.

11. Check carefully for typos, spellos, and other errors. Correct them.

12. Do not put off the task of writing so that it has to be done under time pressures.

1.2. Examples From the Media

As you go through the course, be on the lookout for examples of misleading statements, faulty reasoning, and misuse of data. Look for examples of good thinking, also. Examples can be found everywhere—on labels of products, television advertisements, the editorial pages of newspapers, political statements, and even in college classrooms. Find one example and write a brief discussion of what is wrong or right with it. If it is heard on radio or seen on television, paraphrase what you heard and describe what you saw. For example, what are the claims about "ginseng root" (a popular product found in health food stores)? Is there any evidence that it does what the labels claim that it will do? Numerous advertisements claim that their products will give you more energy or help you lose weight. Should you believe these claims? You could write to the Food and Drug Administration with your conclusions. You could also write to the manufacturer or seller of the product. I think that you'll find this assignment to be fun.

1.3. Journals

Keep a written "journal" that shows your thoughts about the material in each of the chapters. The purpose of these journals is to let you "step back" and reflect on the material that you are learning (Meyers & Jones, 1993). For each chapter, set aside at least two different times when you will think about the material and write your thoughts. There is no single best way to think about these topics. The journal is a record of your discussions with yourself. For example, write down which concepts seem unclear, which seem especially useful, or how you used a particular concept when reading the newspaper or listening to a discussion on the bus or at your kitchen table. This is the time to make your own connections between and within chapters and from class to the "real life" that happens out of class. Add any relevant thoughts that came from class, or another text, or from you. Active reflection on the material you are learning is an excellent habit that will promote critical thinking and long-term retention of the material. There will be space set aside in this exercise book for each chapter where you can record your thoughts. You should find it interesting to review your journal some time in the future. It can provide a snapshot of what and how you are thinking as you go through the text.

Name: **Date:**   **Course/Section:**

Journal Entries

Record your thoughts as you reflect on the material in the introductory chapter. The purpose of this journal is to let you step back and contemplate the material that you are learning. It is a place to record your discussions with yourself. Write about topics that are unclear or seem particularly useful to you. This is the time to make your own connections between and within chapters, from class, and the real life that happens out of class. Use the next page for your second entry.

_____

Date of first entry

Journal—second entry for chapter 1:

_____
Date of second entry

1.4. Thought Process Protocols

Before you start this exercise, either set up a tape recorder or find a friend who will write down everything you say. Presented next is a problem that you can use to practice verbalizing your thought processes. As you work on the problem, say out loud everything you are thinking. This is not a test of how well you think, just a way to help make you more aware of how you approach problems and think them through (Galotti, 1995). It provides an account of your thinking processes that is ordered in time:

BEGIN BY READING THIS PROBLEM ALOUD.

Last semester you were having some difficulty in a math course, and Sarah, who was also in the course, gave you a lot of help so that you could get a good grade in the course. This semester Sarah is taking a computer course, and she is having difficulty learning one of the software packages that is being taught. She has a part-time job and is unable to go to the lab to get extra help because of her work. She has a computer at home, but she does not have the software. She has talked with you about her dilemma several times. You feel obligated to help her in return, but the only way to help her is to make a copy of the software used in class. (Garver, quoted in Miller, Kupsh, & Larson Jones, 1994)

You know that it is unethical to copy the software for this purpose. It is also possible that one of the laboratory assistants will catch you copying it, and then you will have to appear before the university disciplinary committee. You have no idea what the consequences would be if you were caught, but it is unlikely that you would be caught. How do you decide what to do? What would you do?

BEGIN YOUR THOUGHT PROCESS PROTOCOL NOW.

After You Have Thought Through the Problem Out Loud. Now find three other people and ask them to think aloud as they work through the same problem. Be sure to capture everything they say. If they get quiet for a few seconds, prompt them to keep talking. Compare the way each of you worked through the problem. Was there an orderly way in which the various factors were considered? Did you or the others keep returning to one point that was particularly salient to you or to them? Did all of you reach the same conclusion? If not, try to follow each "line of thought" to see how it led to each conclusion.

THOUGHTFUL QUESTIONS

Answer the following questions in the space provided:

1.1. How is critical thinking defined in this chapter? Why does the definition include the notion of likelihood? If you can come up with a better definition for this term, write it here.

1.2. Why was the author critical of the political candidate who opposed waste, fraud, pollution, crime, and overpaid bureaucrats? Shouldn't we be concerned with these issues?

1.3. List several different types of evidence that thinking can be improved with instruction.

1.4. Opponents of critical thinking instruction sometimes say that it's not needed because everyone has a right to his or her own opinion. How did the author respond to this comment? What is your response?

1.5. What is a preferred mode of thought?

1.6. Explain the idea that thinking is done with images and/or verbal statements. Give an example of each.

1.7. In what important ways are humans and computers similar? What are the important differences?

1.8. How can the analysis of thought process protocols help psychologists understand how people think? How can they be used to improve the thinking process?

1.9. What points were raised in this chapter when trying to decide if computers think?

1.10. The answer to the question of whether intelligence can be improved with instruction depends on how intelligence is defined. What are the components of intelligence, and can they be improved with appropriate learning experiences?

1.11. What are some differences in the way good and poor thinkers solve reasoning problems? What are the attitudinal characteristics of good thinkers?

1.12. Explain the notion that critical thinkers are "mindful." What is it that they are mindful of?

1.13. What are the four questions that are being used to provide a framework for critical thinking?

Return to the true–false questions you answered before you read chapter 1. Look over your responses and compare them with the correct answers. Answers: 1. F 2. T 3. F 4. F 5. T 6. F 7. T 8. F 9. T 10.T

SELF-RATINGS OF CRITICAL THINKING SKILLS AND DISPOSITIONS

Evaluate Your Thinking Skills and Dispositions

The purpose of the introductory chapter is get readers to think about their own thinking and to make judgments about their own strengths and weaknesses. Consider each of the thinking skills listed next. Rate your ability with each of the skills using the following scale:

```
 1   2   3   4   5   6   7   8   9   10
extremely poor   average          superior
```

_____ 1. *Recognition, identification, and control of variables*—Recognizing, controlling, or weighing multiple influences in solving problems. For example, interpreting historical phenomena by sorting political and social factors using the available information and deciding whether there are cause and effect relationships or whether variables are too confounded to permit a reliable inference.

_____ 2. *Awareness of gaps in knowledge or information*—Recognizing when you have failed to understand material because you can't establish the meaning of a term or there is incomplete information provided.

_____ 3. *Understanding the need for operational definitions*—Recognizing when a concept has not been clearly defined and the need for using only words with prior definitions in forming a new definition.

_____ 4. *Considering the strength of the reasons that support a conclusion*—Listing the reasons in an argument and considering how well they support a conclusion along with assumptions, qualifiers, and counterarguments that impact on the level of support.

_____ 5. *Drawing inferences from data and evidence, including correlational reasoning*—Considering sample size, measurement, and convergent validity when assessing empirical data.

_____ 6. *Using rational criteria when making decisions*—Listing and weighing alternatives and criteria that are important in reaching a decision.

_____ 7. *Systematically applying a plan for solving problems*—Being consciously aware of problem-solving strategies and applying them systematically when faced with a difficult decision.

_____ 8. *Reading for comprehension*—Monitoring comprehension of difficult text and knowing when to reread and when to skim; includes the frequent use of paraphrase and summaries.

_____ 9. *Concern for accuracy*—Habitually checking work for accuracy and for comprehension.

_____ 10. *Trying creative approaches*—Making the effort to generate novel and useful responses to problems.

_____ 11. *Deliberately using multiple modes of thought*—Trying to think in spatial, verbal, and nonverbal modes.

___ 12. *Working in a planful manner*—Looking ahead and anticipating difficulties when working on a problem.

___ 13. *Communication skills*—Communicating clearly and effectively when speaking and writing.

___ 14. *Recognizing propaganda*—Recognizing propagandistic techniques that are designed as emotional appeals.

___ 15. *Maintaining an open attitude*—Willingness to suspend judgment and to accept a nonpreferred alternative if it is well reasoned.

Look back over your answers. Do you see any patterns of weaknesses or strengths? At the end of this exercise book, you will be asked to rate yourself a second time on these variables. At that time, you can compare the way you answered these questions today with the way you will answer them when you finish the exercises in this book.

2

MEMORY: THE ACQUISITION, RETENTION, AND RETRIEVAL OF KNOWLEDGE

BEFORE YOU READ THE SECOND CHAPTER:
TRUE OR FALSE?

Circle the correct answer.

1. There are many different varieties of memory, each with its own rules for enhancing memory.

T   F

2. If you want to ensure good memory, it is best to study all of the material at one time so that it will be recalled as a single unit.

T   F

3. When people encounter information that is different from their stereotypes, they are more likely to alter their memory for the event than they are to change their stereotypes.

T   F

4. Research on eyewitness testimony has shown that it is usually highly accurate.

T   F

5. Memories that we are unable to retrieve when they are needed (inert memories) are rarely a problem because the information becomes spontaneously available in the presence of any retrieval cue.

T   F

6. A major difference between good and poor learners is knowledge about one's own memory (metamemory).

T   F

7. Most mnemonic techniques require little conscious effort.

                    T   F

8. External memory aids are often the best way to remember.

                    T   F

9. Although psychologists recognize that memory is often biased, there is nothing that can be done to counteract this bias.

                    T   F

10. All information in memory is equally likely to be recalled.

                    T   F

CHAPTER OBJECTIVES

Chapter 2 was written to provide a general overview of how the memory systems work along with a "user's manual" to your own memory system. Several strategies are presented to help the reader learn new material and recall it when it is needed. It is also important to recognize the limitations and biases in memory so that readers are not misled into believing that memory is always highly accurate and to consider the way your failure to recall some information could be biasing your thinking.

Journal Entries

Record your thoughts as you reflect on the material in chapter 2. The purpose of this journal is to let you step back and contemplate the material that you are learning. It is a place to record your discussions with yourself. Write about topics that are unclear or seem particularly useful to you. This is the time to make your own connections between and within chapters, from class, and the real life that happens out of class. Use the next page for your second entry.

_____

Date of first entry

Name: **Date:**   **Course/Section:**

Journal—second entry for chapter 2:

_____
Date of second entry

REVIEW OF MEMORY SKILLS

When you decide that you want to remember something, use some combination of these skills, selecting those that are most appropriate for the task.

<u>When Learning:</u>
    Pay attention.
    Monitor meaning.
    Distribute learning.
    Impose an organization.
    Generate multiple cues for retrieval.
    Overlearn.
    Take care of mental and physical health.
    Assess prior knowledge.
    Assess ease of learning.
    Monitor the acquisition process.
    Use external memory aids, if possible.
    Deliberately use a mnemonic device that is suited for the material you are learning.
    Image when possible.
    Practice motor skills.

<u>During Retention:</u>
    Be aware of the way memories can change.
    Consider inferences and try to separate them from memories.
    Rehearse periodically, if possible.
    Make feeling of knowing judgments.

<u>At Retrieval:</u>
    Beware of overconfidence in memory.
    Examine recall for possible errors.
    Use the cues you generated at learning.
    Keep working at retrieval.
    Make judgments about your confidence in your recall.
    Use the mnemonic strategies that you employed when learning.
    Consult the external aids that you set up at learning.
    Image the information you are recalling.

ACTIVE LEARNING EXERCISES

Try out the memory skills you've learned in this chapter.

2.1. If you are currently learning a second language, use the keyword technique for second-language learning (Atkinson, 1975) to learn your foreign vocabulary for the next month. You may find that it's fun to change the way you usually study, and you should be able to improve your memory for the foreign language terms. If you are not currently studying a foreign language try this with a foreign language you already know. Record the foreign language words and keywords here, and describe the image you are using.

2.2. Now that you understand the importance of attention for memory and thought, try to become aware of the times when your attention wanders from a task. With some effort, you can learn to pay attention. You may be surprised at all that you've missed. The next time you take a walk, notice the colors of the flowers, the shades of raindrops, the expressions of children. Some believe that artists attend to these things that most of us miss.

Record times when you found your attention wandering from a task. Can you discern a pattern in the times that attention wandered? Under what conditions does this seem to happen (e.g., studying at night, in the lecture hall)?

2.3. Observe a classroom, any grade level, and tally the number of times within a 10-minute period that students appear to not be paying attention. What sort of evidence did you use for inferring that someone is not paying attention (e.g., eyes wandering, doodling, glazed look, snoring)? Give two suggestions for maintaining attention.

2.4. Organize your notes so that topics that belong together are placed near each other. Divide your study material into units that can be studied in one block of time. Look for the structure in the material you're learning and interrelate the items so that you can "see the whole picture."

Describe how you used the principles of organization to improve the way you work and learn:

2.5. Go to your local courthouse and observe part of a trial. (Traffic court works well for this purpose.) What are some possible memory biases in the testimony given by eyewitnesses? Do you think that the trial would have had a different outcome if the jurors knew that memory is often unreliable (trials on television can also be used for this exercise)?

2.6. Use the mnemonics described in this chapter to help you prepare for exams. Be sure that you understand the material you're learning.

What mnemonic did you use? Were you successful in improving your retention? Why or why not?

2.7. There are many popular memory games. For example, one game involves planning for a trip. Each person tells what she or he will pack and must also remember what the previous players are packing. Use imagery so that for each item you can visualize it along with the person's face who named the item. You'll be sure to win first prize, unless someone else in the room is also using an imagery mnemonic. What were the results of this exercise?

2.8. Be aware of common notions of memory that are presented in books, on television, and in movies. Most show memory as a passive storage tank that can be accessed with the appropriate tools. Few present the view that memory is dynamic and changes as the individual changes. Discuss these topics with friends and family to see what they think about memory. How do common beliefs about memory differ from the view that is presented in your text?

Describe one example of memory that you found in a book (e.g., Sherlock Holmes), movie, or television show. Is it accurate?

2.9. Try to remember something that happened to you in your childhood and then compare that memory with the account given by a parent or older child you were with at that time. Compare the similarities and discrepancies in your memories. What are some principles that you've learned in this chapter that could account for the differences?

Describe what each of you remembered and how confident each is of her or his memory. Explain your findings.

2.10. Learn how to generate your own retrieval cues. Loftus (1980) suggested that if you go to the supermarket without a shopping list, you can remember what items are needed by going through categories such as dairy, spices, meats, and cleaning supplies. You can use categories as retrieval cues in a variety of situations. Did you ever have the frustrating experience of knowing that you have to call someone, but don't remember whom? Try to recall by systematically going through categories—family, friends from school, employer, etc.

Without consulting any other sources, write out the names of as many of your classmates from high school as possible. When you start "running out of names," think about different places such as clubs, different classes, the lunchroom, etc. Did more names get recalled as you switched locations? Describe what happened. Write the names here as you switch locations.

2.11.   For the following tasks, indicate the type of goal involved and one or more mnemonics that would be useful for the situation described. What should you do when learning and recalling in each of these situations?

a. Studying for a physiology exam that involves learning Latin names for body parts.

b. Remembering where you left your car at the time you park it.

c. Remembering where you left your car hours later when you realize that you can't find it.

d. Considering all of the factors in deciding whether to spend spring break in Florida with friends or with your kid sister in Saskatchewan.

e. Helping a friend remember a joyous childhood experience.

f. Learning the part for a lead role in a school play.

g. Learning a random list of digits in the order in which they were presented.

h. Learning the value of pi to 12 decimal places.

i. Recalling where you were on New Year's Eve.

j. Remembering to stop for a paper on your way home from work.

k. Learning your new telephone number.

1. Learning the main themes in Shakespeare's collected works.

2.12. Find a willing family member, friend, or classmate and help him or her remember what he or she was doing at exactly 5 p.m. last Monday. Describe what you did to improve recall and its result.

2.13. Make 10 copies of Fig. 2.1 that shows two different card hands—one from a poker game and the other from a game of "old maid." Find some friends who are very good at poker and some who are not. Show them each hand, one at a time, for 2–3 seconds and then have them write down the names of the cards that they saw. You should find that the good players recall many more cards correctly for the poker hand than for the old maid hand. There should be little difference in the number of cards correctly recalled for either hand by the not-so-good poker players. Did you get these results? Whether you got them or not, what do the hypothetical results that I just described tell us about the memory of experts? Explain the role of chunking.

FIG. 2.1.   A poker hand and an old maid hand.

2.14.   Read this:

Are you sure that you read it correctly? Did you notice "the the?" Most people don't notice that the word "the" is printed twice. Based on memory and the way it influences what we see, explain why this happens. Show this to several friends and ask them to read it. What percentage fail to see "the the?"

THOUGHTFUL QUESTIONS

Be sure that you can answer the following questions:

2.15. Why should a book on critical thinking skills begin with a chapter on memory? What does memory have to do with thinking?

2.16. What is the relationship among learning, retaining, and recalling? (You should have expected this question.)

2.17. Why are learning and memory called hypothetical constructs? Name two other examples of hypothetical constructs.

2.18. Name and explain some basic properties of attention. Why is it an important concept in memory?

2.19. Several different types of memory were discussed in your text. Briefly describe motor memory, episodic memory, procedural memory, semantic memory, and automatic memory.

Which of these memories is involved when:

learning new vocabulary words?

improving your ability to dribble (in basketball)?

attending a party?

deciding how often you studied your history?

learning how to use Windows on your computer?

2.20. How can stereotypes and prejudices influence what we remember? Describe an experimental study that supports this view.

2.21. What does it mean to say "memory is malleable?"

2.22. How can the development of a good metamemory improve your academic performance?

2.23. What can you do to monitor your own learning?

2.24. How do mnemonic devices work? List and describe four different types of mnemonics.

2.25. Which cognitive principles are used in the cognitive interview? Describe a situation in which this technique would be useful.

Return to the true–false questions you answered before you read chapter 2. Look over your responses and compare them with the correct answers. Answers: 1. T 2. F 3. T 4. F 5. F 6.T 7. F 8. T 9. F 10. F

3

THE RELATIONSHIP BETWEEN THOUGHT AND LANGUAGE

BEFORE YOU READ THE THIRD CHAPTER: TRUE OR FALSE?

Circle the correct answer.

1. In order to communicate clearly, you need to have some knowledge about your audience, for instance, their background knowledge and reason for the communication.

        T   F

2. Analogies usually hinder the communication process because they always involve comparing two things that are fundamentally different.

        T   F

3. The problem in deciding whether "assisted suicide" is murder depends on the way the word "murder" is defined.

        T   F

4. The way we think influences the words we use to express our thoughts; the reverse situation, that is the idea that the words we use can influence how we think, is blatantly wrong.

        T   F

5. The use of prototypes in thinking is usually a deliberate and conscious strategy to help us think creatively.

        T   F

6. Judgments and evaluations about any situation often depend more on the context than on the actual event that is being judged.

        T   F

7. A good way to improve comprehension is to develop the habit of asking and answering thoughtful questions about the material you are learning.

T   F

8. A linear arrangement of facts is too simple an arrangement to be useful when learning new material.

T   F

9. Students who were identified as "at risk" of failing could only improve in their comprehension and memory by reading the material that was to be learned several times.

T   F

10. Graphic organizers aid comprehension because they force the learner to attend to and identify the relationships among concepts.

T   F

CHAPTER OBJECTIVES

The goal of this chapter is to make readers aware of the reciprocal influences of language and thought, so that they can recognize and resist language used in misleading ways. One way to improve the process of thinking is to develop an awareness of the way words direct thinking. For example, the use of analogies as a means of persuasion is pervasive in our language. Conscious thought about the quality of the analogical relationship is needed rather than the unthinking assumption that the analogy is valid. Similarly, many outcomes depend on the way in which a word is defined and who gets to do the defining. Labels, emotional language, and prototypical thinking (thinking with readily available examples) can all cause serious errors in the thinking process. Whether or not we can think critically about a topic depends on what we comprehend. Strategies to improve comprehension are provided so that readers can improve their ability to understand and remember complex material. These strategies must be practiced and used if they are to be effective.

Journal Entries

Record your thoughts as you reflect on the material in chapter 3. The purpose of this journal is to let you step back and reflect on the material that you are learning. It is a place to record your discussions with yourself. Write about topics that are unclear or seem particularly useful to you. This is the time to make your own connections between and within chapters, from class, and the real life that happens out of class. Use the next page for your second entry.

_____

Date of first entry

Name: **Date:**   **Course/Section:**

Journal—second entry for chapter 3:

_____

Date of second entry

REVIEW OF THOUGHT AND LANGUAGE SKILLS

Category description: The skills listed under this rubric include those that are needed to comprehend and defend against the persuasive techniques that are embedded in everyday language (also known as natural language).

Skill	Description	Examples of Use
a. Recognizing and defending against the inappropriate use of emotional and misleading language (e.g., labeling, name calling, ambiguity, vagueness, euphemism, bureaucratese, and arguments by etymology)	This is an assortment of common misleading verbal techniques based on language usage in which a bias for or against a position is created with the connotative meaning of the words used to describe and define the concepts.	Critical thinker (CT) recognizes the use of biased language in numerous contexts such as the following examples: (a) accidental killing of U.S. troops referred to as "friendly fire," (b) use of labels such as "pro-choice" and "pro-life" to create favorable impressions, (c) report of research that "suggests" a finding instead of stating the results, (d) use of the term "disinformation" instead of "lies," (e) calling an opponent a "pinko," (f) using obscure terminology as a way of inhibiting comprehension
b. Detecting misuse of definitions and reification	Both of these techniques are attempts to persuade—the first by assigning arbitrary definitions and the second by treating abstract concepts as though they had an objective reality.	In a discussion of whether alcoholism is a disease, CT knows that the answer depends on the way the term "disease" is defined. A hypothetical construct is defined and then treated as though it were objectively real, such as the use of terms like "self-defeating personality" to attribute blame to women who are battered.
c. Understanding the use of framing with leading questions and negation to bias the reader	A framed question or negation creates an expectation for the type of response that is expected.	CT recognizes the bias in questions like, "Which of the presidential candidates is worse?" (implication that both are bad) and "Don't you agree that the company plan is sure to work?" (bias toward a positive response).
d. Using analogies appropriately, which includes examining the nature of the similarity relationship and its connection to the conclusion	Analogies are effective persuasive techniques—good analogies are based on underlying relationships that are validly transferrable between the analogy and base domain.	In response to a suggestion that welfare recipients serve on welfare boards, a board member replied that this was like suggesting that the mentally retarded serve on the boards for their mental institutions. CT asks if the analogy between the mentally retarded (who cannot act intelligently) and welfare recipients is valid.
e. Employing questioning and paraphrase as a skill for the comprehension of text and oral language	The ability to state a main idea and identify supplementary ideas is essential for comprehension.	An extended presentation is made in which the speaker includes a main idea, supplemental information, and irrelevant information. CT can summarize meaningfully what has been said.
f. Producing and using a graphic representation of information provided in prose form	Converting information from verbal to graphic formats is one measure of comprehension that can be useful in applying the information provided.	Information about a spatial topic such as the plan for a new community is presented in prose. CT can convert the information to a spatial representation. Alternatively, CT can chart relationship information when it is presented in prose (e.g., matrices, hierarchies).

ACTIVE LEARNING EXERCISES

Practice the thought and language skills you've learned in this chapter.

Identify possible attempts to mislead how you think in the following statements. Determine if any of the following are being used: ambiguity, vagueness, emotional terms, equivocation, etymology, framing, bureaucratese, euphemism, reification, and negation. Explain your answers. Which ones are not necessarily misleading, but only might be depending on context? There may be more than one correct answer.

3.1. Why should I have to learn about analyzing arguments to determine if they are clear? Aren't there too many arguments in the world already?

3.2. It is not true that the governor did not oppose a ban on the sale of guns.

3.3. This song is a big hit in Mexico.

3.4. Why would you want to be friends with a queer?

3.5. The best way to overcome shyness is by retraining your personality.

3.6. Druggies hits a higher level of pain relief.

3.7. Only future yuppies would attend that snooty private school.

3.8. The word *education* comes from "educe," which means to bring out. When we educate someone we should be trying to bring out the information that he already knows.

3.9. Pursuant to our agreement and attached hereto is the codicil. (A codicil is an amendment to a will.)

3.10. Have your stomach pains been accompanied by increased flatulence?

3.11. When you purchase new bedroom furniture, delivery is free.

3.12. The Giants are not having a bad season.

3.13. Did you see the car run the stop sign?

3.14. This ground beef is 75% fat free.

3.15. This ground beef is 25% pure fat.

3.16. Coke is it!

3.17. All patriotic Canadians will agree.

3.18. I don't know which of them is worse.

3.19. In a discussion about boxing, George D. Lundberg, a prominent physician, expressed this view: "Boxing is an obscenity . . . a throwback to uncivilized man, and should not be sanctioned by any civilized society" (Lubell, 1989, pp. 126–131).

3.20. The only days that are real holidays are those that are of religious importance because the word "holiday" was derived from the words "holy day."

3.21. Only health nuts and oppressors would favor a ban on smoking.

Consider and comment on the following analogies. How good are they? In what ways are the two topics that are being compared similar and dissimilar? What is the purpose of the analogy?

3.22. You'd go to an orthopedist if you broke your arm, so why not go to a love doctor when you break your heart?

3.23. It is completely legal to drink alcohol and smoke cigarettes, both of which are known to have serious effects on one's health. Yet, marijuana is not legalized, and its effects on health are not as well documented as alcohol and smoking. Therefore, marijuana should be legalized.

3.24. Comprehension is like moving a jungle gym from your friend's yard to your own. (Refer back to the text for the rest of this analogy.)

3.25. Jealousy is a green-eyed monster.

3.26. My love is like a red, red rose.

3.27. Why should the children of faculty members attend the university free? We don't send the children of politicians or public school teachers to school without cost.

3.28. Federal Judge Robert Sweet expressed the following opinion on drug use: "If our society can learn to stop using butter, it should be able to cut down on cocaine" (Bennett, 1990, p.90).

3.29. In an argument on the need to have national tests of what students know, the following analogy was proposed: Tests allow us to determine if the educational system is well or ill; tests are like taking a patient's temperature.

Following are several kinds of text (3.30 through 3.35). Which graphic organizer would you use to depict the underlying relationships? Why? (There may be more than one correct answer.)

3.30. A complex "whodunnit" type mystery story.

3.31. An essay on the effects of geography on the type of economy that develops in a region.

3.32. A manual on the repair of automobiles.

3.33. A description of a chemical chain reaction.

3.34. A classification of wild plants endogenous to Tasmania.

3.35. A "how-to" manual for deep sea diving.

3.36. Use the generic questions that are presented in Table 3.1 in the text for the information provided in this chapter. Write out the questions and respond to them. When you finish, stop to consider if this exercise improved your comprehension.

3.37. Use a graphic organizer to depict the information presented in the chapter on memory (chapter 2).

3.38. Use the strategies for comprehension in your other classwork. If you're not taking any other classes, apply them to a lengthy newspaper or magazine article.

3.39. List at least five situations that would require the deliberate use of strategies for comprehension.

3.40. Draw a flow chart of the information provided in this paragraph:

In the event of fire you should feel the door. If it is hot, remain in your room with the door closed. If the door is cool, open the door carefully and look for smoke in the hall. If there is smoke remain in your room with the door closed. If there is no smoke, proceed to the exit. (Black & Black, 1985, p. 193)

THOUGHTFUL QUESTIONS

Be sure that you can answer the following questions:

3.41. Explain the relationship between underlying representation and surface structure. Why has the gap between them been called the "problem" of producing and comprehending language?

3.42. What is the Sapir–Whorf hypothesis of linguistic relativity?

3.43. Distinguish between the strong and weak forms of the Sapir–Whorf hypothesis. What do you think about the truth of each of these forms?

3.44. Experimental studies were presented to demonstrate empirically how slight changes in wording can cause substantial differences in the way people think. Describe two of these studies.

3.45. What are some circumstances when it is particularly important to consider the way choice of words influence thought?

3.46. What's wrong with interpreting the meaning of a word by reference to its origin?

3.47. How do you decide which strategy to improve comprehension should be used?

3.48. What general cognitive principles are common to all of the strategies for improving comprehension?

Comment on the following statements. Explain what is wrong with each, if there is something wrong. If it seems okay, then say so. Remember, not every communication is misleading.

3.49. I recently heard a discussion that went something like this: Because every society has always consisted of a vast majority of people who are heterosexual, it follows that homosexuality is not normal.

3.50. There is a wide range of products that have been marketed as "clear." We now have clear colas among other products. The ads tell us that the products are "so pure, that they are clear." (There are so many clear products, I expect to see clear ketchup and gravy.)

3.51. In the 1988 presidential debate between Michael Dukakis and George Bush, Dukakis told Bush that he was branding women who seek abortions as criminals. The next morning, Bush's campaign manager said that Bush prefers to think of women who seek abortions as "additional victims" (Seech, 1993).

3.52. Gynecologists have traditionally considered themselves as medical specialists—a title that brought increased prestige and money over that of a "generalist" physician. Under a health plan that is being considered, "primary-care physicians" (a fancy term for a generalist) would receive additional pay. The gynecologists are now arguing that they really are primary-care physicians.

3.53. The publisher of a sexually explicit newspaper, Alexei Kostin, was jailed in Moscow, Russia for publishing pornography. This arrest was in accord with a criminal code that prohibits pornography. However, the code (Article 228) never defines pornography (from Mac Kenzie, 1994).

3.54. Vladimir Zhirinovsky, leader of an "ultranationalist" political party in Russia, has denied that he is anti-Semitic, although he does believe that all Russian Jews should be forced to leave Russia and that they should not be allowed to hold responsible or influential jobs.

3.55. According to a radio news broadcast (British Broadcasting Company, 1994), tourist guides in Virginia have added a new attraction. Tourists now see "old Southern mansions." Formerly, these sites were called "plantations."

3.56. In a study reported by Cialdini (1993), college students rated average-looking females and males as less attractive after viewing a television show with beautiful people than if they watched a different show.

3.57. Explain the term "risk adverse." Write two different hypothetical advertisements for insurance (any type), one that uses the principle that most people are adverse to risk and one that does not use this principle. Compare the two. Does the advertisement that is based on risk adversion seem more persuasive? Explain the differences between your two advertisements.

Return to the true–false questions you answered before you read chapter 3. Look over your responses and compare them with the correct answers. Answers: 1. T   2. F   3. T   4. F   5. F   6. T   7. T   8. F   9. F   10. T

4

REASONING: DRAWING DEDUCTIVELY
VALID CONCLUSIONS

BEFORE YOU READ THE FOURTH CHAPTER:
TRUE OR FALSE?

Circle the correct answer.

1. The rules of logic can be used to win any argument.

T   F

2. In many real-world settings, people switch between deductive and inductive reasoning.

T   F

3. Asking if Tiffany is taller than Kart is pragmatically the same as asking if Kart is shorter than Tiffany.

T   F

4. According to the formal rules of logic, content should be important when deciding if an "if, then" reasoning problem is valid.

T   F

5. If a prosecutor is able to prove beyond a reasonable doubt that a crime occurred at a time when the defendant does not have an alibi, we can conclude that the defendant is guilty.

T   F

6. The statement that "some politicians favor gun control" means the same thing as "some politicians do not favor gun control."

T   F

7. Truth and validity mean the same thing.

T   F

8. If we believe "if guns are outlawed, then only outlaws will have guns," then it would be logical to believe that "if guns are not outlawed, then people other than outlaws will have guns."

T   F

9. When people test their personal beliefs about the world, they tend to seek information that supports their beliefs instead of information that runs counter to their beliefs.

T   F

10. A good way to change attitudes is to present many statements, followed by evaluations of the statements so that a conclusion is implied.

T   F

CHAPTER OBJECTIVES

The purpose of this chapter is to enhance the deductive reasoning skills of readers and to provide practice with several different types of diagrams that can be used with many types of problems. The skills developed in this chapter are most similar to those used in college-level mathematics as they provide a single correct answer and require careful consideration and execution of all steps in the process. Deductive reasoning is based on the assumptions that if certain information is true, then there are conclusions that must also be true.

Both spatial and verbal strategies are used to help readers practice both modes of thinking. Common biases and errors in deductive reasoning are introduced. Many of these are discussed in several other chapters using different perspectives. The use of deductive reasoning skills in real-world contexts is also highlighted so that readers can recognize when deductive reasoning skills are needed and when they are being persuaded with deductive reasoning techniques.

Journal Entries

Record your thoughts as you reflect on the material in chapter 4. The purpose of this journal is to let you step back and reflect on the material that you are learning. It is a place to record your discussions with yourself. Write about topics that are unclear or seem particularly useful to you. This is the time to make your own connections between and within chapters, from class, and the real-life that happens out of class. Use the next page for your second entry.

_____

Date of first entry

Name: **Date:**   **Course/Section:**

Journal—second entry for chapter 4

_____

Date of second entry

Review of Deductive Reasoning Skills

Category Description: The skills presented in this chapter are used to determine if a conclusion is valid—that is, it must be true if the premises are true. These skills are used in many contexts including law, medicine, financial projections, and the sciences.

Skill	Description	Example of Use
Discriminating between inductive and deductive reasoning	Recognizing the differences between using beliefs and deciding what to believe	Inferring attitudes from behaviors (inductive) and predicting behaviors from someone's stated attitudes.
Identifying premises and conclusions	Being able to recognize what is being advocated and the reasons for it	Reading a ballot issue and knowing the position that is supported and why it is being supported
Using quantifiers	Understanding the use of terms like "every," "some," and "not"	Knowing that "doctors recommend" means "some doctors recommend"
Understanding the difference between truth and validity	Knowing that a conclusion can be valid, but false	It may be valid to believe that welfare spending should be increased given a set of premises, but the premises and the conclusion may be wrong.
Using syllogisms to change attitudes	Following premises with evaluative statements that support a belief	For example, "Juveniles commit many crimes. They need alternatives to crime. So, fund activities for juveniles."
Watching for marked adjectives	Marked adjectives bias evaluations	"How dumb is he?" is not a neutral question.
Reasoning with "if, then" statements	Understanding what is and is not implied in "if, then" statements	"If you learn the skills, your thinking will improve," but it may improve even if you don't.
Working with disjunctives	Being able to determine what is implied with "or" statements	Either you'll go to class or you won't pass the exam.
Examining everyday contexts for missing quantifiers	Knowing, for example, that "all" is implied, but "some" is meant	Pharmacists do not have the knowledge to determine if drugs interact. This should be a "some" statement instead of the implied "all."
Using linear ordering principles	Being able to arrange objects along a dimension	Kalin arrived before Joe or Roberto, but after Alexie. Who arrived first?
Avoiding the fallacy of denying the antecedent and confirming the consequence	In "if, then" reasoning, premises that deny the "if" part or affirm the "then" part often lead to errors	If you reduce your fat intake, you will be healthier. You did not reduce your fat intake. What can we conclude?
Using circle diagrams to check category membership	Combining class membership categories to determine what can be concluded	Some high school students studied Latin. All students who studied Latin went to college. Can we conclude that some high school students went to college?
Using tree diagrams	Learning how to draw branches and nodes to represent information	If Sara is home, she's on the phone. Sara is on the phone. Is she home?

ACTIVE LEARNING EXERCISES

Try out the reasoning skills you have learned in this chapter.

I. Use the appropriate diagrams to select the valid conclusion or conclusions. Check your work with the rules for syllogisms where it is appropriate. Don't be confused by the fact that several different conclusions are presented for each problem. If you draw on a set of diagrams, you should be able to decide which, if any, of the conclusions is valid.

4.1. Some baseball players are scholars.
       No blondes are baseball players.
       Therefore:
       1. All blondes are scholars.
       2. Some blondes are scholars.
       3. No blondes are scholars.
       4. All of the above are invalid.

4.2. All cats are animals with nine lives.
All animals with nine lives are mammals.
Therefore:
1. All cats are mammals.
2. Some cats are mammals.
3. No cats are mammals.
4. All of the above are invalid.

4.3. No presidents are young.
     All young people like Laverne and Shirley.
     Therefore:
     1. No presidents like Laverne and Shirley.
     2. All presidents like Laverne and Shirley.
     3. No people who like Laverne and Shirley are presidents.
     4. All of the above are invalid.

4.4. Carl is smarter than Abby.
      Dan is smarter than Bruce.
      Carl is smarter than Dan.
      Who is smartest?
      Who is dumbest?

4.5. The dog is to the left of the rooster.
      The newt is to the right of the rooster.
      The hyena is to the left of the giraffe.
      The newt is to the left of the hyena.
      Which animal is on the right?

4.6. Which of these conclusions is valid?

If gun control reduces violent crime, then people will vote for it.

People are voting against gun control.

Therefore:

1. Gun control reduces violent crimes.
2. Gun control does not reduce violent crime.
3. No definite conclusion.

4.7. If the Lakers were second, the 76ers came in first.

The Lakers were second.

Therefore:

1. The 76ers came in first.
2. The 76ers did not come in first.
3. No definite conclusion.

4.8. If Robin doesn't phone home, her parents worry.
Her parents are worried.
Therefore:
1. Robin didn't phone home.
2. Robin phoned home.
3. No definite conclusion.

4.9. If Edna doesn't practice, she won't play well.
She doesn't play well.
Therefore:
1. Edna doesn't practice.
2. Edna does practice.
3. No definite conclusion.

4.10. Curly threw the pie or Larry didn't eat it.
Larry ate it.
What can you conclude?

II. The following deductive reasoning problems are embedded in language, the way they normally would be encountered in the real world. Remember, the task here is to assume that the premises are true and then determine what can validly be concluded.

4.11. "Mrs. Cooke had studied home economics in college. 'Youth is a time of rapid growth and great demands on energy,' she said. 'Many youngsters don't get enough vitamins in their daily diet. And since some vitamin deficiencies are dangerous to health, it follows that the health of many of our youngsters is being endangered by inadequate diet.' (Does it follow that the health of many youngsters is being endangered by inadequate diet? Give your reasoning)" (Henle, 1962, p. 371).

4.12. When you use the toothpaste with "sex appeal," you will have more dates than you ever dreamed possible. Your brother bought generic toothpaste (definitely not the one with "sex appeal"). What will using generic toothpaste do to your social life? (This is a paraphrase of a television commercial.)

4.13. The drug problem will not be solved if we legalize drugs. Therefore, we must not legalize drugs. What can we conclude will result from not legalizing drugs? What can we conclude about legalizing drugs?

4.14. You have a new job at a local store. It is your job to go through checks at the end of each day and make sure that any check over $30 has been approved by the manager. The amount of the check is written on the front, whereas the approval is initialed on the back of each check. Which of the following checks below must you turn over to be sure that the sales clerk followed this rule and had checks over $30 approved? (This problem is adapted from Cheng, Holyoak, Nisbett, & Oliver, 1986. I tried a version of this problem when I was teaching at Moscow State University in Russia. It provided a good example of my own ethnocentric biases. Most of the students did not understand the problem because they don't use checks in Russia.)

~~~~~$35 | OK, *dfh* | | ~~~~~$22

4.15. There are random patterns of sound waves emanating from outer space. This must mean that there is life on other planets because if there is life on other planets, then the life forms would be trying to contact us. If they were trying to contact us, then we would be able to pick up random patterns of sound waves.

Is this valid reasoning? Draw the appropriate diagram. Note that you have to go slightly beyond the diagrams that are presented in the text to solve this problem.

4.16. Sometimes illogical reasoning serves as the basis for prejudice. During the Kuwait invasion, I heard the following argument being made: Hussain does bad things (e.g., invade Kuwait, used chemical warfare against dissident groups). Hussain is Muslim. Therefore, Muslims are bad. Determine if this is a valid conclusion. Show all work.

4.17. This is a true story: I was talking to a colleague and I told him that I had taken out student loans when I was in college. He replied that he heard about people like me. He read in the newspapers that many students didn't repay their school loans, so I must be a deadbeat. Was he right? (Be sure that you come up with the right answer. This is critical to my reputation.)

4.18. Suppose that you overheard this conversation: Tiana wants to run for president, and anyone who wants to be a politician is not to be trusted. Therefore, Tiana cannot be trusted. Is this a valid conclusion?

4.19. There is a television commercial for a law firms that goes something like this:

Our law firm is as trustworthy as Abraham Lincoln. Lincoln charged low rates and advertised in the newspapers. We charge low rates and advertise.

Notice that this advertisement begins with the conclusion. Is it a valid conclusion given the two premises? Explain your answer.

4.20. Consider the four cards below (adapted from Wason, 1969):

Every card has a triangle on one side and a circle on the other. Every card that has a black triangle on one side has a blank circle on the other side. Your task is to indicate which of the cards you need to turn over in other to find out whether this rule is true.

4.21. Present the four-card selection task that is presented in the text to your family and friends. Keep track of the percentage of people who select the correct answer as well as other combinations. Explain the correct answer to them.

4.22. Find examples of valid and invalid reasoning from the newspaper, television, billboards, and conversations. If their reasoning is invalid, explain what is wrong with it. Use circle diagrams to check on the conclusions in syllogistic arguments.

THOUGHTFUL QUESTIONS

Be sure that you can answer the following questions:

4.23. Are the psychological processes that people use in formulating conclusions the same ones that are specified by the laws of formal logic? How do they differ? (This should provide a helpful hint for the first question.)

4.24. Why is the legal process described as an "exercise in reasoning?"

4.25. What is the difference between inductive and deductive reasoning? Give an example of each. If you are a fan of the fictional detective, Sherlock Holmes, you should be able to describe one example of each from the famous stories that chronicle his adventures.

4.26. If you need to give someone information about the distance the planets are from the sun and each other, what rules about communicating ordered information do you need to keep in mind?

4.27. What is the difference between truth and validity? Can a conclusion be both? Neither?

4.28. What are the parts of "if, then" reasoning problems? What errors are common when reasoning with them?

4.29. How does negation affect our ability to reason well?

4.30. What is a syllogism?

State the mood for each of the following premises:

> No drugs are good.
>
> Some dogs can't bark.
>
> All birds have feathers.
>
> Some junk food is good.

4.31. Explain what circle diagrams are. Why are they used?

4.32. What are the rules of syllogisms?

4.33. Define the terms "middle term" and "distributed."

4.34. How does content affect the way we reason with syllogisms? How does this differ from the rules of logic?

4.35. How do probability and logic interact to influence our belief in the validity of conclusions?

4.36. Confirmation bias is a ubiquitous effect. What is it? How is it demonstrated in the "four-card selection task?" Explain the correct answer to this problem.

4.37. If you need to try all combinations of five items, two at a time, three at a time, four at a time, and five at a time, how do you form the combinations?

4.38. Why is B distributed in "No A are B," but not distributed in "All A are B?" Explain this.

Return to the true–false questions you answered before you read chapter 4. Look over your responses and compare them with the correct answers. Answers: 1. F 2. T 3. F 4. F 5. F 6. F 7. F 8. F 9. T 10. T

5

ANALYZING ARGUMENTS

BEFORE YOU READ THE FIFTH CHAPTER:
TRUE OR FALSE?

Circle the correct answer.

1. If all people would learn the skills of analyzing arguments, then there would be no more disagreements.

          T   F

2. If you can think of any reasons why a conclusion is false, then you should decide that the conclusion is false.

          T   F

3. When you add weak support to a conclusion, you strengthen the quality of the argument.

          T   F

4. Sometimes, one strong reason that supports a conclusion is "good enough" to believe in the conclusion.

          T   F

5. Rationalizing is a good way to judge the quality of an argument.

          T   F

6. Propaganda is almost always based on false reasons.

          T   F

7. With a little care, it should be easy to tell the differences among facts, opinions, and reasoned judgments.

          T   F

8. In visual arguments, the verbal portion is more persuasive than the more subtle visual elements.

T   F

9. Fallacies can be identified by checking the rules for sound arguments and deciding if any have been violated.

T   F

10. The rules for changing beliefs can be used to check your own arguments for persuasiveness.

T   F

CHAPTER OBJECTIVES

The purpose of this chapter is to help readers learn how to recognize and evaluate arguments and how to spot fallacies that are used in unsound reasoning. Virtually every human interaction involves an attempt to persuade, so it is critically important to understand and use the skills of argument analysis. Readers are expected to learn how to analyze arguments, diagram their structure, and make reasoned judgments about the truth of a conclusion. The same rules of argument analysis also serve as a guide for writing and preparing oral arguments. It is difficult to fool people when they use the criteria for judging the strength of an argument. Historical examples, newspaper editorials, advertisements, and propaganda are used to show the widespread applicability of these rules. Historical atrocities and personal tragedies could have been avoided, if only the populace were given the skills and the freedom to analyze arguments.

Journal Entries

Record your thoughts as you reflect on the material in chapter 5. The purpose of this journal is to let you step back and reflect on the material that you are learning. It is a place to record your discussions with yourself. Write about topics that are unclear or seem particularly useful to you. This is the time to make your own connections between and within chapters, from class, and the real life that happens out of class. Use the next page for your second entry.

_____

Date of first entry

Name: **Date:**   **Course/Section:**

Journal—second entry for chapter 5:

_____

Date of second entry

Review of Argument Analysis Skills

Argument analysis skills are those skills that are needed to judge how well reasons and evidence support a conclusion. They involve considering counterevidence, stated and unstated assumptions, and the overall strength of the argument.

Skill	Description	Examples of Use
Identifying premises (reasons), counterarguments, and conclusions	An argument is an attempt to persuade a listener or reader with at least one reason and one conclusion.	We must increase Social Security benefits because they have not kept pace with inflation. But, some elderly are rich and don't need an increase.
Making strong arguments that show good thinking and communication skills	Arguments should be structured so that the reasons support what is being advocated.	When writing an essay against the death penalty, the writer can identify her own reasons and counterarguments and judge their relative strength.
Judging the credibility of an information source and knowing the difference between expertise in factual matters and in value matters	Judgments of credibility and bias are central to determining the quality of information. Credible sources have expertise, firsthand knowledge, and no basis for gain.	The executives of a car company tout the safety features of their new model car. A veterinarian argues for the use of animals in research.
Understanding the differences among opinion, reasoned judgment, and fact	Opinion is an unsupported preference; reasoned judgment is a conclusion based on reasons for believing it; facts have verifiable truth values.	CT can recognize the differences among: "Unions are needed for the protection of workers, and that's a fact." "Sugar-Os is a good cereal because it contains fiber." "I love the way Sugar-Os taste."
Recognizing and avoiding common fallacies such as straw person, slippery slope, and arguments against the person	There are many common fallacies—deliberately weak arguments, claims that X is true because there is no disconfirming evidence, association arguments.	We cannot ban semiautomatic weapons because all guns will be banned once we start. The health plan is bad because the conservatives support it. Ghosts must exist because no one can prove that they don't.
Identifying psychological effects on reasoning	The appearance of a reason or an irrelevant reason can affect beliefs about a conclusion.	"I need a raise because I need more money." "Pastazoola is a kosher product and because I do not observe kosher laws, I'll pick the other brand."
Remembering to consider what could be missing from an argument	The most persuasive information may be omitted, either deliberately or accidentally.	"Candidate Dogooder is great because he is kind to his dog." Is other information omitted like he is a convicted rapist?

ACTIVE LEARNING EXERCISES

Diagram and evaluate the soundness of the following statements using the steps for analyzing arguments. Be sure to bracket and number the statements before you draw the diagrams. There may be more than one correct way to diagram complex arguments.

5.1. The reason we have so many juvenile delinquents is that there are too many working mothers.

5.2. She looked deep into his baby blue eyes and proclaimed, "I love you."

5.3. You really should consider becoming a physics major. The topic is interesting and there are plenty of good jobs available.

5.4. You really should consider becoming a physics major. The topic is interesting and there are plenty of good jobs available. With a wide range of available jobs, you probably could find a job near your home town. Of course, it will require lots of hard work. Physics is a particularly good choice for students who enjoy the sciences and mathematics. Students with math anxiety probably won't be happy as physics majors.

5.5. Eighteen-year-olds should not be allowed to drink because they are too young.

5.6. The trade agreement between Mexico and the United States is needed in order to improve the skiing in Colorado.

5.7. There is too much violence shown on the network channels. Advertisers will only pay for shows that have large viewing audiences, and these tend to be shows with excessive sex and violence. For this reason, a public television station supported by tax dollars is needed. But is it fair to make all taxpayers contribute to public television stations when most don't watch them? We believe that it is. Without tax-supported public television, we will never be able to provide high-level television programming. (This is a more difficult passage. You may have to paraphrase the meaning of a statement. Start by identifying the conclusion, and then the reasons that support it and the counterarguments.)

5.8. The classic books of Western civilization are the building blocks of our society. Very few college students will read them unless they are required to. For these reasons, these books should be required reading for all college students.

5.9. Are you tired of the way politicians are running this country? If so, vote for me. Remember, when you vote for Elvira Slick, you're voting for me.

Part B. For each of the following examples, indicate if a fallacy is being committed, and if so, label it and explain why the reasoning is fallacious. (More than one fallacy may apply.) Whenever you decide that a line of reasoning is fallacious, you should be able to explain why.

5.10. How can the U.S. Supreme Court decide that high school newspapers can be censored when papers written by those not in high school cannot be censored? Nothing magical happens the day someone graduates from high school. Students are only 1 day older. We can't have laws that apply to you one day and different laws that apply the next day.

5.11. I wanted to buy a Jaguar but I couldn't afford it, so I bought a Ford instead.

5.12. "At last, four new residences designed to delineate a new level of luxury. Some visitors will find the opulence disturbing. Perhaps you will recognize a unique opportunity. From one-half million dollars . . . " (quote from an advertisement for condominiums, *The Los Angeles Times*, 1983).

5.13. Of course, the new senator will be conservative. His father and mother are conservatives, and his brother-in-law is head of "Conservatives for Better America."

5.14. We can only conclude that there is no such phenomenon as extrasensory perception because no one has been able to demonstrate that it exists.

5.15. "Your Honor, you should judge this young girl not guilty of the crime because she came from a broken home."

5.16. California State University is the best school for you. It has a better computer major than Colorado State and is cheaper than Harvard.

5.17. This diet is doctor tested and approved!

5.18. Over the past 50 years, all U. S. wars occurred while we had a Democratic administration. "I would ask [Senator Kennedy] to name one Republican president that led this country into war." (This sentence was spoken by Richard Nixon during a televised debate.)

5.19. Walter Cronkite buys his clothes at Snooty Brothers. He's a man who knows. Shouldn't you be shopping here, too?

5.20. You'll get better tasting cake with Happy Homemaker Cake Mix.

5.21. We can either send troops to the Middle East or pull out entirely. Which course of action do you prefer?

5.22. What will I do to improve the union now that I've been elected president? Why, I'll do anything I can to make it better.

5.23. The committee to investigate the causes of Alzheimer's disease will surely be able to find the cause because the committee is composed of leading researchers in the field.

5.24. The question of whether we should allow gay fraternities to meet on campus is easy to answer. How would you like it if your son joined a gay fraternity?

5.25. The problem of incest is a serious one for contemporary society. There has been a dramatic increase in the number of unreported cases in the last several years alone.

5.26. You want to change the way we do business around here? Well, I believe that if it ain't broke, don't fix it.

5.27. "More Californians are choosing Bank of America because we have more automatic teller machines" (taken from a television commercial).

5.28. The United States should not be sending troops to South America. We sent troops to Viet Nam and the outcome was very poor.

5.29. It is stupid to believe that the United States should stay out of South America.

5.30. We cannot believe that genetic engineering is safe because the researchers are atheists.

5.31. We cannot believe that genetic engineering is safe because the researchers have a substantial profit motive that may override their concern for safety.

5.32. Marijuana is a serious threat to society. College enrollment has declined at a rate that is the same as the rate of increase in marijuana consumption.

5.33. He is a poor writer because his essays are badly written.

5.34. Wrinkle-away cream is the fastest way to reduce wrinkles around the eyes and mouth.

5.35. You really should take Professor Snodley's class because enrollment in his class is low.

Part C: Carefully consider the following statements. For each statement, decide if it is an opinion, reasoned judgment, or fact. If it is a fact, decide if it is an important or relevant one.

5.36. Bold has a new and improved formula to get clothes even whiter.

5.37. The new formula in Soapies is effective in removing spinach and grass stains; therefore, Soapies' new and improved formula will get clothes even whiter than the previous formula.

5.38. Speedo is a faster acting cold remedy.

5.39. Tang has more vitamin C than plain orange juice.

5.40. Pearl Gray is the best candidate for the job!

5.41. Josh is the best pitcher on the team.

5.42. Josh hit more home runs than anyone else on the team.

5.43. Josh is the best pitcher on the team. He was the only pitcher to pitch a no-hitter.

5.44. Ray got 80% of the arithmetic problems correct.

5.45. Druggies hits a higher level of pain relief.

5.46. In a taste test with over 100 dogs, 3 out of every 4 dogs preferred the taste of Crunchies brand dog food. Doesn't your dog deserve the best?

5.47. Diamonds are a good investment.

5.48. Interest rates have dropped 3 percentage points since March.

5.49. The national debt must be reduced.

5.50. As free Americans, we have the right to bear arms.

5.51. George Washington was the first president of the United States.

5.52. Historians who have examined paintings of George Washington have concluded that he didn't have wooden teeth.

5.53. Vegetarian diets can reduce certain health risks.

5.54. Vegetarians have low cholesterol levels. It seems likely that vegetarian diets can reduce certain health risks.

5.55. Here are three "person on the street" answers to the question, "Should the Catholic Church Throw Out Its Rule on Celibacy for Priests and Nuns?" (1994). Compare the reasoning. What assumptions are being made? These responses are verbatim.

21-year-old student: "Yes. You can be married to someone as well as to the church; then priests, nuns could better experience real life. And marriage would help solve the problem of child abuse by priests; it's caused by pent-up emotions that are channeled in abnormal ways."

33-year-old customer service representative: "It's difficult to answer, because I'm a practicing Catholic, *but* people are going to be people, and we have these urges! If they could marry, priests wouldn't bother little boys, and nuns wouldn't slap the little kids in grammar school."

46-year-old retired officer: "Yes. Love, marriage; it's the nature of life. I am from Jordan, and I am Catholic. I've asked many priests how they survive as men. They say if they pray they can get rid of 'evil' thoughts. One priest I know has a secret life with a woman; he prays a lot."

5.56. Keep a record of the persuasive techniques that appear on billboards, radio, and television. A particularly good source for this material is the solicitations for political and charitable organizations that are mailed to your home. Letters to the editor in newspapers and cartoons also rely on common persuasive techniques to "make their point."

5.57. There are many different proposals for improving public education. One proposal is to double funding. Formulate your thoughts on this question. Then, fill in the following format:

State your conclusion:
Give three reasons that support your conclusion, and rate each one for how well it supports your conclusion. Use weak, moderate, strong, or very strong as your rating scale.

a.

Rating for a:

b.

Rating for b:

c.

Rating for c:

Give two counterarguments that weaken your conclusion, and rate each for how much it weakens your conclusion. Use little, moderate, much, and very much to rate how much it weakens your conclusion.

a.

Rating for a:

b.

Rating for b:

If your argument involves any assumptions list them here:

Now diagram the argument that you just made, and give it an overall rating of its strength.

Can you see how this sort of exercise is a good way to organize your thinking before you write a persuasive essay?

THOUGHTFUL QUESTIONS

5.58. Why does Harmon call reasoning "a change in view?"

5.59. How do convergent argument structures differ from chained structures? What is the net effect on the strength of the argument if I add a weak premise to each of these argument structures?

5.60. How do you determine if a premise is acceptable? What standards should you be applying?

5.61. What do you need to consider when assessing the credibility of an expert? Why is the credibility of an expert an important factor in determining the acceptability of a premise?

5.62. Explain the concept of relatedness as it applies to the relationship between a premise and a conclusion.

5.63. What are the criteria for a sound argument?

5.64. Why is it important to consider what's missing from an argument when you evaluate its soundness?

5.65. Explain the experiment that was described in the section on the psychology of reasons. Under what circumstances were people willing to let someone go ahead of them when waiting in line?

5.66. What is the effect of irrelevant reasons on the choices that we make? Why do irrelevant reasons influence thinking?

5.67. The 21 common fallacies are based on unsound reasoning. Which ones are examples of premises that are unrelated to the conclusion?

5.68. How does reasoned judgment differ from opinion? Give an example in which an opinion serves as a premise in an argument.

5.69. How do you change someone's beliefs?

5.70. What criteria should you use to judge the arguments that you are making?

5.71. How can visual stimuli be used to support or weaken a conclusion?

Return to the true–false questions you answered before you read chapter 5. Look over your responses and compare them with the correct answers. Answers: 1. F 2. F 3. T 4. T 5. F 6. F 7. F 8. F 9. T 10. T

6

THINKING AS HYPOTHESIS TESTING

BEFORE YOU READ THE SIXTH CHAPTER:
TRUE OR FALSE?

Circle the correct answer.

1. An important difference between inductive and deductive thinking is that you can prove your beliefs with the inductive method, but you can only provide support for your beliefs with the deductive method.

    T   F

2. Sample size is an important variable in both formal scientific research and in casual observations about the nature of the world.

    T   F

3. A careful report from a single individual whom you know is often more reliable than a study that used many subjects.

    T   F

4. When we make judgments about groups of people, we tend to think of people in groups that we don't belong to as being very similar to each other and people in the groups we belong to as being very different from each other.

    T   F

5. In determining cause, the most important variable is the use of correlated groups.

    T   F

6. One problem with retrospective research is that memory is biased.

    T   F

7. A negative correlation is undesirable because it shows the negative effect that one variable has on the other.

T   F

8. The Rorschach (ink blot) test has been criticized because of the problem of illusory validity.

T   F

9. Ben Franklin never said, "Experience is the best teacher."

T   F

10. It is a good idea to find a therapist who has had the same problems as you have because this person will have especially good insight on how to overcome the problems.

T   F

CHAPTER OBJECTIVES

The objective of this chapter is to help readers improve the way they understand causal relationships and events that occur together. The scientific methods of testing hypotheses are applied to understanding everyday events so that we can all use them as a lay method to understand our day-to-day world. Readers are expected to understand why it is critical to consider the size of a sample, the people who make up the sample, the possibility of confounding, and the way common cognitive biases affect what we recall and we how evaluate information. The skills reviewed in this chapter are important when we act as consumers of formal research such as deciding if secondhand smoke poses a significant health risk and in understanding personal events such as deciding if caffeine causes headaches. The use of the skills of hypothesis testing need to be practiced and used whenever we assess claims of drug effectiveness, the value of social programs, or deciding if any variable is the cause of another.

Name: **Date:**   **Course/Section:**

Journal Entries

Record your thoughts as you reflect on the material in chapter 6. The purpose of this journal is to let you step back and reflect on the material that you are learning. It is a place to record your discussions with yourself. Write about topics that are unclear or seem particularly useful to you. This is the time to make your own connections between and within chapters, from class, and the real life that happens out of class. Use the next page for your second entry.

_____

Date of first entry

Name: **Date:**   **Course/Section:**

Journal—second entry for chapter 6

_____

Date of second entry

REVIEW OF THINKING AS HYPOTHESIS-TESTING SKILLS

Category Description: The skills used in thinking as hypothesis testing are the same ones used in scientific reasoning—the accumulation of observations, formulation of beliefs or hypotheses, and then using the information collected to decide if the information collected confirms or disconfirms the hypotheses.

Skill	Description	Examples of Use
a. Recognizing the need for and using operational definitions	An operational definition is an explicit set of procedures that specify how to recognize and measure a construct.	An advocate for a group claims that child abuse is increasing at an alarming rate. CT will ask how child abuse has been defined and measured.
b. Understanding the need to isolate and control variables in order to make strong causal claims	In determining cause, a single variable is manipulated and the results attributed to that variable are compared to comparable control groups in which the variable was not manipulated.	A commercial states that cholesterol levels were reduced when a group began exercising and using margarine. It concludes that margarine use reduces cholesterol. CT notes the confounding of exercise and margarine use and does not attribute the drop in cholesterol to margarine.
c. Checking for adequate sample size and possible bias in sampling when a generalization is made	Valid generalizations from samples can be made only when the sample size is adequately large (relative to the variability) and the sample is representative of the population.	As part of a conversation, a young adult states that she knows that old people like to watch Lawrence Welk because her grandmother did. CT recognizes that this sample is too small and biased for generalizations about all old people.
d. Being able to describe the relationship between any two variables as positive, negative, or unrelated	Two variables are positively related when increases in one occur concomitantly with increases in the other, negatively related when increases in one occur concomitantly with decreases in the other, and unrelated when changes in one variable are independent of changes in the other.	A newspaper article states that over the last 10 years marijuana use has steadily increased and Scholastic Achievement Test scores have decreased. CT can describe this as a negative relationship.
e. Understanding the limits of correlational reasoning	Although a significant correlation between two variables can suggest that changes in one variable cause change in the other variable, this is weak evidence for determining cause.	A social scientist shows that there has been steady increase in the number of single-parent families and in the number of crimes committed by juveniles over the last 15 years. She concludes that single-parent families are responsible for the increase in juvenile crime. CT notes that these data are correlational and cannot be used to determine cause.

ACTIVE LEARNING EXERCISES

Practice the thinking as hypothesis-testing skills that you've learned in this chapter.

6.1. According to Einhorn and Hogarth (1978), Benjamin Rush, a professor at the first medical school in the United States, believed that "blood-letting" (bleeding) of patients would cure a variety of illnesses. When his patients recovered from their illnesses, he would attribute their recovery to the practice of blood-letting. (Sometimes leeches were used to draw the blood.) When his patients died, he concluded that the nature of their illness was so severe that not even blood-letting could help them. Using your hypothesis-testing skills, comment on Rush's observations and conclusions.

6.2. Whenever someone celebrates his 100th birthday, newspaper reporters ask him to reveal the secret of longevity. Suppose that you read in the newspaper that a 100-year-old man attributed his long life to drinking a bottle of gin a day. Can you conclude that drinking gin will help you to live long?

6.3. Although research has shown that salt-free diets lower blood pressure, Mike doubts that this is true. Mike's father has been on a salt-free diet for over a year and his blood pressure has remained high. What would you say to Mike about his conclusions?

6.4. Jim is very superstitious. He believes that when a black cat crosses his path, something bad happens. What would you tell Jim about his superstition?

6.5. You've probably heard a commercial that goes something like this, "Seven out of 10 dentists recommend Chewsy Gum for their patients who chew gum." Comment on this commercial. What would you want to know in order to evaluate this research claim?

6.6. A conservative group of politicians attempted to persuade the local school board to eliminate its kindergarten program. A study conducted in a rural area of Montana showed that children who went to kindergarten did not score higher on an achievement test than children who did not attend kindergarten. How would you refute or prove their claim that kindergarten is a useless year?

6.7. The question of whether joint custody (custody of the child shared between both parents) is the best arrangement for children following the divorce of their parents has been a topic of considerable concern. Legal hearings on this topic will frequently have one or two families for whom joint custody either worked or didn't work testify about their experiences. Comment on this practice. How would you go about deciding whether or not joint custody is a generally good idea?

6.8. How would you decide if a new reading program should be implemented in your elementary schools?

6.9. Rosenthal and Jacobson (1968) told teachers that some of the children in their classrooms were ready to "bloom" intellectually. As you might expect, the children who were identified as bloomers did show large increases in intelligence. This is especially interesting in light of the fact that there were no real differences between the "bloomers" and other children. They had, in fact, picked the "bloomers" at random. What phenomenon discussed in this chapter can describe this result? How did it happen?

6.10. In a study by Pickren and Gamarra (1975), the following relationship was found between histiocytes in lung tissues and people's smoking histories:

	Total Number of Cases	Cases With Histiocytes
Nonsmokers	31	0 (0%)
Former smokers	38	10 (27%)
Smokers	43	40 (93%)

What can you conclude about the relationship between histiocytes and smoking history? Can you claim that smoking causes histiocytes? Why or why not? (Don't worry if you don't know what histiocytes are. It's not important in answering the question.)

6.11. A mad scientist taught his pet fly to "fetch" a small stick whenever a whistle was blown. The scientist then found that after he cut off the fly's wings, the fly didn't "fetch" the stick. He concluded that flies hear with their wings and that the fly had become deaf as a result of losing its wings. How would you convince the scientist that his experiment doesn't prove that flies hear with their wings? What went wrong with the scientist's thinking?

6.12.   Your friend just returned from a trip to a foreign country. During his trip he became ill and a friendly family helped him to find a doctor and get the medicine he needed. Now he can't stop talking about the friendliness of the people he met there. In fact, he plans to drop out of school, sell his home, and move to this country. Interpret his experience and his conclusion about the people of this country using the hypothesis-testing skills developed in this chapter. Comment on his hypothesis, sample size, measurement, perception about "other group" variability, error "badness," etc.

6.13.   How would you apply double-blind procedures to test the claim that biofeedback can reduce the severity and frequency of migraine headaches? What sort of evidence would you need to decide that migraines can be relieved with biofeedback?

6.14.   A television commercial for a brand of cheese claims that their cheese is best for use in microwaves because it melts quickly. To demonstrate their point, the actors show that the cheese melts faster than a frozen popsicle. Comment on this "experiment."

6.15. A colleague (Dr. Gregory Kimble at Duke University) had a conversation with a taxi driver in New York. The driver told him that he trusted the weather predictions in the *Farmer's Almanac* because whenever it predicted rain, it would usually rain either on the predicted day or a few days before or after the predicted day. What do you think about the nature of this evidence? Does this show that the *Farmer's Almanac* is usually correct in its weather predictions? Why or why not?

6.16. In a classic journal article, a researcher (Dawes, 1979) argued that interviews are too biased to be used as a way of selecting people for jobs or for deciding who should be allowed to enter a university. He suggested that we rely on statistical models of who will succeed and do away with personal interviews. Comment on this suggestion. How would you respond to someone who laments that he was rejected and the committee never even met him, but relied instead on his test scores, grade point average, and essay?

6.17. Over 70% of the people who responded to a write-in survey said that there is too much violence on television. This should send a strong message to television programmers. Comment on this finding. If you were a television executive, would you take this as a mandate to reduce televised violence?

6.18. Think about the television, radio, and magazine advertisements that bombard our daily existence. Collect some "choice" advertisements and question their claims and conclusions. How should they have tested their product?

THOUGHTFUL QUESTIONS

Using the questions for evaluating research claims that are summarized at the end of this chapter, critically discuss each of the following:

6.19. How is everyday thinking like the experimentation used by scientists?

6.20. What is the difference between inductive and deductive methods? How are they used in a cyclical fashion?

6.21. Why do we need operational definitions?

6.22. What are some mistakes that we can make when generalizing from a sample to a population? Describe a better sampling technique than the one used by the *Literary Digest*.

6.23. Explain how confounding can lead to erroneous conclusions. Provide an example.

6.24. List three pairs of variables that you would expect to be positively correlated, three that you would expect to be negatively correlated, and three that you would expect to be uncorrelated.

6.25. Why can't we determine cause from correlated variables? Why is the three-stage experimental design a better method than correlation for making strong causal claims?

6.26. Why do people persist in believing in the validity of their conclusions even when their confidence is unwarranted?

6.27. Why is prospective research preferable to retrospective research?

6.28. We can be more confident in our conclusions when there is convergent validity. Why? If you have already read chapter 5, compare the notion of convergent argument structures with convergent validity.

6.29. Explain why people sometimes believe that variables are correlated when, in fact, they are not.

6.30. How can experimenter and subject biases affect the results obtained from experiments? How do double-blind procedures protect against these biases?

Return to the true–false questions you answered before you read chapter 6. Go over your responses and compare them with the correct answers. Answers 1. F 2. T 3. F 4. T 5. F 6. T 7. F 8. T 9. T 10. F

7

LIKELIHOOD AND UNCERTAINTY

BEFORE YOU READ THE SEVENTH CHAPTER:
TRUE OR FALSE?

Circle the correct answer.

1. Clever gamblers are able to use the "laws of chance" to select winning lottery numbers.

        T   F

2. The purchase of insurance is a type of "bet" that you hope to lose.

        T   F

3. When unusual events occur (e.g., you recover from a terminal illness), we can conclude that something other than luck was responsible.

        T   F

4. When taking a five-alternative multiple-choice test, you are as likely to get all of the questions correct just by guessing as you are to get all of the questions wrong just by guessing.

        T   F

5. Basketball players tend to shoot in streaks so that a player who has just made a basket is more likely to make a basket on her second throw than if she had just missed the basket.

        T   F

6. Your evil twin just took a college entrance exam and scored very, very low. If he takes it again, he will probably obtain an even lower score on his second try.

        T   F

7. Most people assess the risk of elective surgery (e.g., a "nose job") as being safer than nonelective surgery.

T   F

8. If a method of contraception has a 6% failure rate, then you would expect the same probability of getting pregnant in 1 year of use as you would in 10 years of use.

T   F

9. Suppose that your friend plans to become a professional drummer and only 2% of all people who want to become professional drummers actually achieve this goal. In addition, suppose that he has "connections," and 80% of all successful drummers have connections like his. Only 10% of unsuccessful drummers have the same sort of connections. This means that his probability of success would increase slightly above 2%.

T   F

10. Differences between samples don't mean that there are real differences between the groups being sampled unless the differences are statistically significant.

T   F

CHAPTER OBJECTIVES

This chapter discusses the use of likelihood and uncertainty in daily life, the common errors people make when interpreting probabilities, and practical ways to make probabilities understandable. The goal is to make readers aware of the many times they need to think probabilistically about an event and to encourage the habit of estimating likelihoods and questioning statistics. Common errors in thinking statistically are explained including differences among measures of central tendency, the biases that occur when deciding which risks are "too risky," and how to estimate the probability of an undesirable outcome when we are faced with new technologies.

Name: **Date:**   **Course/Section:**

Journal Entries

Record your thoughts as you reflect on the material in chapter 7. The purpose of this journal is to let you step back and reflect on the material that you are learning. It is a place to record your discussions with yourself. Write about topics that are unclear or seem particularly useful to you. This is the time to make your own connections between and within chapters, from class, and the real life that happens out of class. Use the next page for your second entry.

_____

Date of first entry

Name: **Date:**   **Course/Section:**

Journal—second entry for chapter 7:

_____
Date of second entry

REVIEW OF LIKELIHOOD AND UNCERTAINTY CRITICAL THINKING SKILLS

Category Description: The correct use of objective and subjective estimates of probability is an important critical thinking skill because virtually every life event is probabilistic.

Skill	Description	Examples of Use
a. Recognizing regression to the mean	An extreme score on some measure is most likely followed by a score that is closer to the mean.	It is a common phenomenon that a star "rookie" who excels in his or her first season performs closer to average in the second season. CT recognizes that this is an example of regression to the mean.
b. Understanding and avoiding conjunction errors	The co-occurrence of two or more independent events is less likely than the occurrence of either one alone.	Physicians describe the typical heart attack victim as male and over 55. CT realizes that the typical heart attack victim is more likely to be either male or over 55 than both male and over 55.
c. Utilizing base rates to make predictions	The initial or a priori proportion of some group in the population is a valid guide for predicting likelihoods.	A speaker meets a "quiet man who is good with numbers." The speaker concludes that this man is more likely an accountant than a farmer. CT knows that the number of accountants in the population is small relative to farmers and predicts farmer as the more likely occupation.
d. Understanding the limits of extrapolation	Extrapolation is using trends in data to make estimations of future events, a process that is meaningful only if it is not extended too far in time and other factors can be assumed to remain constant.	The population council concludes that based on current birth rates, there will be no resources to feed the multitudes by the year 2050. CT knows that the extrapolation is based on the assumption that there will be no changes in contraception, fertility practices, or food resources.
e. Adjusting risk assessments to account for the cumulative nature of probabilistic events	The probability of one or more unlikely events occurring increases with time and with the number of events.	A physician explains that there are 10 possible side effects of a drug. CT understands that the probability of having 1 side effect is higher when there are 10 possible side effects than if only 1 side effect were possible.
f. Thinking intelligently about unknown risks	New risks can be considered by using historical data, calculating the probability of component parts, and using analogies.	A chemical warfare plant is planned for your community. CT can think about risks by looking at other similar plants, estimating component risks, and using analogies from other chemical plants.

ACTIVE LEARNING EXERCISES

Practice the likelihood and uncertainty critical thinking skills that you've learned in this chapter.

7.1. There is an advertisement that appears on late-night television that offers to sell the secrets to picking winning lottery numbers. The advertisement tells viewers not to play the lottery in a stupid way. Is it possible to play the lottery intelligently by paying for the secret numbers, or is this "bunk?" Explain your answer.

7.2. Suppose now that you learn that most people pick important dates in their life when they select lottery numbers (e.g., birthdays, anniversaries). Could you increase the amount of money that you could win by picking numbers that do not correspond to dates such as numbers greater than 31? Would this system make you more likely to win? Would this system make it more likely that you would win a big jackpot, if you did win? Explain your reasoning. (I thank Dr. Dale Berger at Claremont Graduate School for suggesting this problem.)

7.3. If each of the letters in the word "PROBABILITY" are thrown separately into a hat and one letter is drawn from the hat, what is the probability that it is a vowel? ("Y" is a vowel in this example.)

7.4. Your friend is willing to give you 5:2 odds that the Phillies will beat the Dodgers. Convert these odds to a probability value.

7.5. A. What is the probability of drawing a picture card (jack, queen, or king) from a full deck of 52 cards? B. What is the probability of drawing two aces in a row from a full deck (without replacement)?

7.6. In a party game called "Spin the Bottle," the players form a circle with a bottle at the center. A spinner spins the bottle and then kisses the person to whom it points. Although five people are playing, the bottle has pointed to Marlene on each of its three spins. What is the probability of this occurring by chance? Can you make any "guesses" about Marlene?

7.7. Professor Aardvark gives such difficult exams that students can only guess at the answers. A. What is the probability of getting all five questions on his true–false test correct by guessing (assuming that every alternative is equally likely to be correct)? B. What is the probability of getting all five wrong?

7.8. Rubinstein and Pfeiffer (1980) suggested that instead of reporting weather forecasts in terms of the probability of rain, a more useful index would be the Expected Value (EV) of rain. Suppose the weather forecaster knows that there is a 30% probability of 5 inches of rain and a 70% probability of no rain on a given day. What is the EV for rain? Is this number more useful than the probability of rain?

7.9. Officials at the suicide prevention center know that 2% of all people who phone their hotline actually attempt suicide. A psychologist has devised a test to help identify those callers who will actually attempt suicide. She found that 80% of the people who will attempt suicide attain a positive score on this test, but only 5% of those who will not attempt suicide attain a positive score on this test. If you get a positive identification from a caller on this test, what is the probability that he would actually attempt suicide?

Hint: Set up a matrix like the one shown below and then fill in the appropriate numbers.

Score	Will Attempt Suicide	Will Not Attempt Suicide	Row Total
Positive Score			
Negative Score			
Column Totals			

Draw a tree diagram with four branches, multiply along the branches, then form the correct ratio. The numerator will be the proportion that would actually attempt suicide and the test predicts that they will score *over* this number plus the proportion that do not attempt suicide and the test predicts that they will. Follow the example in the book for José, if you're having trouble getting started.

7.10. Every student in Mr. Weasel's class kept a record of the number of books read over a 3-month period. The data are: 15, 5, 8, 12, 1, 3, 1, 7, 21, 4. Compute the mean and median for these numbers. Which one seems better as a measure of central tendency?

7.11.   Abby scored very low on her SATs. Her score of 350 is well below the mean of 500. If she retakes the test, which of the following is most likely to occur and why did you pick that answer?

a. She will probably score below 350.
b. She will probably score close to 350.
c. She will probably score between 350 and 500.
d. She will probably score near 500.
e. She will probably score above 800.

7.12.   A gourmet critic found that she is frequently disappointed when she returns to restaurants that she found to be outstanding on her first visit. She concludes that the chefs get lazy over time and do not put as much effort into their cooking. What do you think about her reasoning?

7.13.   When the College Board announced that, on the average, males score somewhat higher on the mathematics portion of the test, Darryl protested. His sister scored a perfect 800 on this test and his girlfriend scored "way better" than he did. Comment on Darryl's protest.

7.14. You joined an office "pool." There are eight teams that you can bet on. You bet on the mighty Coyotes which have won 40% of the games played so far this season. You decided to bet $5.00 on them. If you lose, you lose your $5.00. If you win, you get back your $5.00 and get another $5.00. If you bet on the Coyotes all season and the probabilities remain the same, what is the expected value of each bet? How much should you expect to win or lose if you bet on 10 games?

7.15. You are planning on a beautiful picnic. You will only go on your picnic if it doesn't rain, and your friend goes with you, and the park is open. The mean old weather forecaster is predicting a 40% chance of rain. Not only that, but your friend is only 75% sure that he will go with you. The park ranger is 90% sure that the park will be open this time of year. What is the probability that it won't rain, and your friend will go with you, and the park will be open (assuming independence)? Before you start this problem, estimate your answer.

7.16. How certain can we be about the occurrence of an event if its probability is 0? .2? .5? .9? 1.0?

7.17. You were just thinking about an old friend from high school when your mother walks into the room and tells you that she bumped into this old friend. Isn't this amazing? Don't you think that you can use this example to convince your skeptical friends that you have ESP? Explain your answer.

THOUGHTFUL QUESTIONS

7.18. Explain how Al Hibbs was able to "beat the house" at roulette.

7.19. What is the logic of tree diagrams? Explain what you are doing when you draw tree diagrams.

7.20. What principle explains why the probability of 40 people sharing a common birthday is as high as .90? Explain it in words.

7.21. Explain gambler's fallacy. What is fallacious about it? Ask your friends what they would expect on the next flip of a fair coin that has landed "heads up" on the last five flips. Why did I call the belief in streaks the "flip side" of gambler's fallacy?

7.22. When people were asked to judge the frequency of lethal events, what kinds of errors did they make?

7.23. If a disease is very rare (i.e, it has a very low base rate), how optimistic can we be about devising a test that will detect it? Why?

7.24. If a student gets the highest grade in his class on a psychology exam, what grade would you predict that he will get on the midterm? What is the name of the principle you used to make this prediction?

7.25. Explain why the Israeli flight instructors believed that praise led to poorer performance and criticism improved performance. What is a better explanation of these results?

7.26. Give two examples of situations is which tree diagrams can be used as decision-making aids.

7.27. Every time I buy an appliance, the salesperson tries to sell me product insurance. I always decline and explain to the salesperson that, in the long run, I am better off never buying appliance insurance for small appliances because the cost of the insurance is calculated so that I would be expected to lose money. This is how the companies make money on the insurance. Often a salesperson will argue with me and tell about a customer who got a brand new replacement appliance when his broke down and was still under warranty. Explain why the "expected value" for the consumer is always negative. How would you explain these concepts to a friend who is contemplating the purchase of insurance? Why should I buy auto insurance, even though, it, too, has a negative expected value for all consumers? (Think about the amount of risk.)

7.28. How are conjunctive errors evidence that many people don't understand the reasoning behind the "and" rule? I have had students who found it very difficult to understand why Linda, the example in the book, is more likely to be a bank teller than she is to be a bank teller and a feminist. I often will draw circle diagrams to explain this relationship. Try this demonstration with friends and then explain the correct answer to them.

Return to the true–false questions you answered before you read chapter 7. Go over your responses and compare them with the correct answers. Answers 1. F 2. T 3. F 4. F 5. F 6. F 7. T 8. F 9. T 10. T

8

DECISION MAKING

BEFORE YOU READ THE EIGHTH CHAPTER:
TRUE OR FALSE?

Circle the correct answer.

1. Once you have decided on an alternative, it is best *not* to review your decision because research has shown that the first choice most people make is usually the best.

        T   F

2. It is usually not possible to determine if the best decision was made.

        T   F

3. If we develop the habit of writing lists of alternatives on paper, then we don't have to be concerned about the possibility that memory is biasing the decision-making process.

        T   F

4. When people are highly confident about their ability to make sound decisions, their self-confidence is usually warranted.

        T   F

5. We tend to judge information that is easy to recall as more frequent in occurrence than information that is difficult to recall.

        T   F

6. When picking six lottery numbers, 12, 7, 4, 31, 6, 28 is more likely to win (if the lottery is fair) than 1, 2, 3, 4, 5, 6.

        T   F

7. When you are deciding about continuing a project in which you have already invested time and money, the amount of time and money that you have previously invested should be the primary consideration.

T   F

8. The fact that you are familiar with something or someone will influence your decision so that the alternative or person is evaluated more favorably than a less familiar alternative or person.

T   F

9. There is a considerable body of evidence that shows that people make better decisions when they use a worksheet procedure.

T   F

10. A decision should always be judged by the quality of its outcome.

T   F

CHAPTER OBJECTIVES

This chapter examines how people typically make decisions in day-to-day situations and provides a model for improving the decision-making process. Several common fallacies or errors in decision making are explained along with ways to avoid them. The objective of this chapter is to help readers make better decisions by avoiding common errors and using good techniques that are known to improve the probability of a sound decision. A decision-making worksheet procedure is presented that will help readers with the important decisions in their lives.

Name: **Date:**   **Course/Section:**

Journal Entries

Record your thoughts as you reflect on the material in chapter 8. The purpose of this journal is to let you step back and reflect on the material that you are learning. It is a place to record your discussions with yourself. Write about topics that are unclear or seem particularly useful to you. This is the time to make your own connections between and within chapters, from class, and the real life that happens out of class. Use the next page for your second entry.

Date of first entry

Name: **Date:**   **Course/Section:**

Journal—second entry for chapter 8:

_____

Date of second entry

Review of Decision-Making Skills

Category Description: The skills used in decision making are those used in framing a decision, generating and evaluating alternatives, and analyzing the outcome.

Skill	Description	Examples of Use
a. Framing a decision in several ways to consider different sorts of alternatives	The deliberate use of different ways of phrasing a decision that needs to be made.	Changing the wording in a decision such as "How can we provide low-cost health care to everyone?" to "How can we reduce the cost of quality health care?"
b. Generating alternatives	Coming up with several possible ways to satisfy the goals of the decision.	Two alternatives are: 1. Provide incentives to keep health care costs down. 2. Add basic medical information to high school curricula.
c. Evaluating the consequences of various alternatives	Thinking through likely and unlikely results of different alternative solutions.	The incentive system for health care might reduce the quality of the care. Giving everyone better health education could prevent some illness.
d. Recognizing the bias in hindsight analysis	Hindsight analysis is the reevaluation of a decision after its consequences are known.	After a parolee kills someone, many people want to fire the parole board. CT knows that the decision may have been reasonable at the time it was made.
e. Using a decision-making worksheet	It is a procedure for listing alternatives and important considerations and then calculating a decision.	In deciding what to do about a revolution, the leaders could list possible actions, analyze and weigh them, and then calculate a decision.
f. Avoiding the entrapment bias	Entrapment occurs when a course of action requires additional investments beyond those already made.	Shana decides to stick with her boyfriend who treats her badly because she has already invested several years in the relationship.
g. Seeking disconfirming evidence	There is a pervasive bias to seek information that confirms what we believe to be true.	Make a conscious effort to find information that would not support the decision to have children when you are inclined to have children.
h. Awareness of the effects of memory on decisions	We generate alternatives and decisions that we can easily recall.	Seek a variety of input when deciding which college to attend.

ACTIVE LEARNING EXERCISES

Try out the decision making skills you've learned in this chapter.

8.1. Think of a major decision that you will be facing in the near future. Use the worksheet procedure to help you reach a decision.

8.2. Study a major political decision that was made in the last 25 years (e.g., the Bay of Pigs decision, Watergate, President Ford's decision to pardon former President Nixon, the decision to offer arms to Iran in exchange for hostages, the decision to send troops to Somalia). Look for the role that fallacies and heuristics played. Analyze the decision. Based on the information that was available at that time, would you have made the same one? If not, what would you have done?

8.3. Look for instances of the confirmation bias, availability heuristic, representativeness heuristic, wishful thinking, cognitive dissonance, and hindsight in the everyday decisions made by yourself and others around you. List an example that you found and explain how the example fits the definition given in the text.

8.4. Reread the hospital scenario presented at the beginning of this chapter. Based on what you've learned about how to make sound decisions, what would you do if you were the protagonist in this story?

8.5. Try out some of the examples presented in this chapter on your friends (e.g., the ascending number series, the multiplication series, the information about a symptom and disease, the head–tail sequence). If they make the usual errors, explain to them why the errors occurred and how to avoid these errors in the future. Describe what happened.

8.6. Consider the political candidates who are running in a current election, or select a past election. Use the process of elimination by aspects to decide which candidate is best. Explain the process.

Comment on the following:

8.7. "We've already invested over \$2 million of taxpayer funds in this project. If we pull out now, all that money will be wasted."

8.8. "Of course Ngyuen will make a fine class president. He always says nice things to me."

8.9. "No, we're not prepared for a flood. Although we had a serious flood last year, another one is not likely to happen."

8.10 "Italians are naturally musical. After all, where do you think Frank Sinatra came from?"

8.11. "I'm sure that their next child will be a girl. After all, they already have six boys."

8.12. "It's a good idea to use 'Goniffs Are Us' for investment advice. Last year they recommended that their clients invest in Bob's Bank and that turned out to be an excellent investment."

8.13. "I think that there is no reason to require motorcycle riders to wear a helmet, but I do believe that we should have strict laws regarding recombinant DNA because it's so risky."

8.14. "After all the work Loren put into selecting the right phone company, the company he selected was subject to a corporate takeover, and now we're stuck with poor phone service. He would have been better off if he'd just flipped a coin."

8.15. "Of course, the decision to 'take' the Davidian compound was stupid. Don't you remember the massacre at Jonestown?"

8.16. Your neighbor believes that men like more aggressive sports and women like more artistic sports. He polled several people in the neighborhood and found that out of the 100 neighbors (59 women and 41 men) he polled, 29 of the men and 24 of the women preferred wrestling to ballet. The rest expressed the opposite preference. Do these data support your neighbor's belief? Explain your answer.

8.17. Compare these two sets of questions:

a. Does the continent of Asia contain more or less than 10% of the world's population?

More   Less

What percentage of the world's population is contained on the continent of Asia?

b. Does the continent of Asia contain more or less than 80% of the world's population?

More   Less

What percentage of the world's population is contained on the continent of Asia?

The only difference between A and B is in the value given in the more or less question. In A, the value is 10%. Most people will respond "more" to this question. In B, the value is 80%. Most people will respond "less" to this question. Ask the A questions to five people and the B questions to another five people. What is the average answer given when they have to estimate the percentage? What do you think that you will find? Why? Did you get the results you anticipated? Explain how the values 10% and 80% influenced estimates of an unknown figure.

THOUGHTFUL QUESTIONS

8.18. Describe two experimental studies that support the validity of the worksheet procedure.

8.19. What are heuristics? How do they differ from algorithms? Describe two examples of heuristics. Are they necessarily bad? Are they sometimes bad?

8.20. List and describe the steps in preparing a decision worksheet.

8.21. How does the theory of cognitive dissonance explain why people are usually satisfied with the decisions they make?

8.22. Explain how the "elimination by aspects" strategy can be applied to deciding where to live.

8.23. What should a decision maker do if one alternative "wins" by the overall assessment method and a different one "wins" by the dimensional comparison method?

8.24. How can the "failure to seek disconfirming evidence" lead to wrong decisions in research?

8.25. Justify all of the effort involved in making a worksheet.

8.26. How could a decision worksheet be a valuable aid to people in psychotherapy?

8.27. Explain how psychological reactance can cause people to select a less desirable alternative.

8.28. How does reciprocity influence the kinds of choices we make?

8.29. Why is hindsight a detrimental process? Why does the author state that sometimes good decisions will have detrimental outcomes? If the outcome is bad, doesn't that mean that the decision was bad?

8.30. What sort of information should you have when making a decision about a potential risk?

8.31. Describe a study of the effect of mood on decision making.

8.32. Explain how memory can affect decision making.

Return to the true–false questions you answered before you read chapter 8. Go over your responses and compare them with the correct answers. Answers 1. F 2. T 3. F 4. F 5. T 6. F 7. F 8. T 9. T 10. F

9

DEVELOPMENT OF PROBLEM-SOLVING SKILLS

7. Conflict problems are especially amenable to strategies that require each side to assume the perspective of the other side.

T   F

8. The culture in which we grew up can have important influences on the way we define and solve problems.

T   F

9. A mechanized approach to problem solving is always bad because it does not encourage the consideration of problems in novel ways.

T   F

10. Expertise can be judged most accurately by the amount of experience a person has at a certain task.

T   F

CHAPTER OBJECTIVES

This chapter explores what makes up a problem and the kinds of strategies and techniques that can be useful in helping you solve problems. In addition, several types of obstacles that may impede finding solutions to problems are discussed. The goal of this chapter is to make readers more aware of the options they have in finding, defining, and solving all sorts of problems. Specific plans are presented that can be used with almost any problem. They are especially useful when you have a problem and you have no idea how to begin the process of devising a solution. If you practice the skills presented in this chapter and use them when you encounter problems in real life, you should become a better problem solver.

Journal Entries

Record your thoughts as you reflect on the material in chapter 9. The purpose of this journal is to let you step back and reflect on the material that you are learning. It is a place to record your discussions with yourself. Write about topics that are unclear or seem particularly useful to you. This is the time to make your own connections between and within chapters, from class, and the real life that happens out of class. Use the next page for your second entry.

_____

Date of first entry

Name: **Date:**   **Course/Section:**

Journal—second entry for chapter 9:

_____

Date of second entry

Review of Problem-Solving Skills

Category Description: The skills used in problem solving are those that are needed to identify and define a problem, state the goal and generate and evaluate solution paths.

Skill	Description	Examples of Use
a. Restating the problem and the goal to consider different sorts of solutions	Most real-life problems are ill-defined; that is, there are many possible goals and ways to achieve them.	Several ways of increasing sales are described. CT redefines the problem to include other ways to increase profits (e.g., cut inventory).
b. Recognizing the critical role of persistence	One of the best predictors of success when solving problems is persisting until a good solution is found.	When encountering a difficult problem, CT doesn't quit when a solution is not immediately obvious, but keeps working on it.
c. Using a quality representation of a problem (e.g., graphs, trees, matrices, and models)	Visual representations of problems can assist with comprehension and serve as problem-solving aids.	A problem is described verbally. The task for the CT is to depict the information in a graphic display in order to solve it.
d. Understanding worldview constraints	The problems we identify and how we solve them are influenced by our culture.	CT learns from other cultures in order to increase problem-solving repertoire.
e. Selecting the best strategy for the type of problem	There are many different strategies that can help solve problems; CT knows how to select from among them.	A problem involving categories of information is approached with a matrix, which is well suited for this sort of problem.
f. Actively seeking analogies	Problems concerning very different topics can involve similar solutions.	In order to recognize an analogous solution, CT actively seeks analogies by using visualization and other analogy techniques.

ACTIVE LEARNING EXERCISES

Try out the problem-solving skills you've learned in this chapter.

9.1. A frog fell into a 5-foot deep well and needs to begin the arduous task of hopping out. Every hour he jumps 2 feet, but then slides back 1 foot. How long will it take him to get out of the well? (Hint: Draw a diagram.)

9.2. Irvin has begun a jogging program. He jogs 2 miles north, then turns right and jogs 3 miles, then heads left 1 mile, then turns and jogs 2 miles to the right, then he jogs 3 miles south, and finally 5 miles west. How far is he from his starting point? (Hint: Draw a map.)

9.3. You agree to be a contestant on a silly television show. There are 24 gift boxes lined up in four rows of 6 boxes each. One of these boxes contains the grand prize (a weekend in San Bernardino, California). You can ask your television host any question that has a "Yes" or "No" answer. What questions would you ask him? How many questions would you need to definitely identify the box containing the grand prize? (Hint: Use the strategy that works best with an organized array of equally likely choices.)

9.4. There are four dogs sitting in front of their dog houses. The dogs, in left-to-right order, are Pizza, Tiger, Lady, and Sancho. Based on the information given next, figure out which dog eats Crunchy Blend dog food.

1. Pizza lives in a blue dog house.
2. The dog who lives in a red house eats Yummies.
3. Sancho eats Butcher Boy dog food.
4. Lady lives next to the dog with the green house.
5. Tiger lives next to the dog who eats Crunchy Blend.
6. The dog in the white house is next to the dog who eats Butcher Boy.
7. The dog who eats medium rare steak is farthest away from the dog who eats Butcher Boy.

(Hint: Use the form of representation that is recommended when the givens are taken from categories of information.)

9.5. Solve the following anagrams:

CRA   NTU   ETA   NIK

(Hint: Use the strategy that is recommended for problems with few solution paths.)

9.6. Design an automobile that can drive across land and water.

9.7. Using Fig. 9.1, place the cowboys on their horses so that they can ride properly. (Hint: You will have to break set to answer this problem.)
The answer is presented at the end of the chapter.

FIG. 9.1. Can you figure out how to place the cowboys on their horses so that they could ride properly? (From M. Scheerer, Problem solving © 1963 by Scientific American, Inc. All rights reserved.)

9.8. Using only six short sticks, arrange them to form four equilateral triangles. (Hint: This problem will also require that you break a mental set.)

9.9. The notched-checkerboard problem: "You are given a checkerboard and 32 dominoes. Each domino covers exactly two adjacent squares on the board. Thus, the 32 dominoes can cover all 64 squares on the checkerboard. Now suppose two squares are cut off at diagonally opposite corners of the board (see Fig. 9.2). Is it possible to place 31 dominoes on the board so that all of the 62 remaining squares are covered? If so, show how it can be done. If not, prove it impossible" (Wickelgren, 1974, p. 29). (Hint: This problem is directly analogous to another one solved in this chapter.)

FIG. 9.2. The notched checker-board problem. (After Wickelgren, 1974, p. 29.)

9.10. The Jealous Husbands Problem: "Three jealous husbands and their wives, having to cross a river at a ferry, find a boat. However, the boat is so small that it can hold no more than two people. Find the simplest schedule of crossings that will permit all six people to cross the river so that no woman is left in company with any of the men unless her husband is present. It is assumed that all passengers on the boat get off before the next trip and that at least one person has to be in the boat for each crossing" (Reed, 1982, p. 308). (Hint: This problem is directly analogous to another one solved in this chapter.)

9.11. A favorite of Newell and Simon's (1972) is this crypt arithmetic problem:

```
 D O N A L D
+G E R A L D
 R O B E R T
```

The problem is to substitute a digit (0 through 9) for each letter so that the letters follow the usual rules of addition. (Hint: D = 5.) I'll demonstrate the first step:

```
 5 O N A L 5
 G E R A L 5
 R O B E R O
```

I'll give you a second hint: R must be an odd number. Complete this problem.

9.12. Complete the following letter series. (This problem has been used in intelligence tests for English schoolchildren.)

OTTFFSS—

What are the next three letters? (Hint: Thinking about repeating sequences of letters will lead to blind paths.)

9.13. An anxious mother wants to send a T-square (a rigid drafting instrument) to her son in college. The T-square is 13" long. Unfortunately the express mail service won't accept any packages more than 12" long. How was she able to send the T-square by express mail? (No, she didn't cut or fold it. Hint: Draw boxes around an imaginary 13" T-square.)

9.14. A penny gum machine is filled with red and white gumballs. There is no way of knowing the color of the next ball. If Mrs. Jones wants to be sure of getting a matching pair of gumballs, how many pennies must she be prepared to spend (Gardner, 1978)? (Hint: This problem is analogous to another one presented in this chapter.)

9.15. A man bought a horse for $60 and sold it for $70. Then he bought it back again for $80 and sold it for $90. How much money did he gain or lose on these transactions? (Hint: Think about different ways to rephrase the problem.)

9.16. "If one greyhound can jump over a ditch 2 meters wide, about how wide a ditch can six greyhounds jump across?" (Bereiter, 1984).

9.17. The alphabet is presented next in two rows. What is the rule that determines whether a letter belongs in the top or bottom row?

A   EF   HI KLMN   T VWXYZ

BCD G   J   OPQRS U

9.18. Here is a classic problem that appeared in a longer form in Ann Landers' advice column (January 13, 1992):

Dear Ann: My wife and I soon will be celebrating our 30th wedding anniversary, and although we've been quite happy together, I can't bring myself to tell my wife something that's been bothering me since our honeymoon. Louise never told me that she played the accordion and that she took it with her everywhere. I was flabbergasted on our honeymoon night as I sat through three recitals of "Lady of Spain" and an old English madrigal with surprisingly ribald lyrics. Those are the only tunes that she knows.

Our social life has always been quiet. Our only friends are Bernice and Murray. They come over quite often and join Louise in a rousing chorus of "Lady of Spain." Murray plays his head—that is, he raps his knuckles on his head while opening and closing his mouth, which produces changes in tone. Bernice clacks two spoons together and hums the harmony.

Ann, the racket is driving me crazy. Any suggestions?

In thinking about this problem, decide if it can be stated with at least four different goal states. For each goal state, come up with at least two possible solutions. When you are finished, decide if you have hit upon a good solution. I have presented Ann Landers' solution at the end of this chapter. Decide if the solution you decided on is as good as hers.

9.19. Find problems of your own and apply the strategies you've learned in this chapter.

THOUGHTFUL QUESTIONS

9.20. Identify and explain the "anatomical" parts of all problems.

9.21. What are the four stages in problem solving? How does each stage contribute to the solution?

9.22. Give an example of a well-defined and an ill-defined problem. In general, how do they differ?

9.23. How are external forms of representation (e.g., graphs, diagrams) helpful in solving problems?

9.24. List five different problem representations and explain when each is most likely to be useful.

9.25. Explain how persistence can be a useful problem-solving aid.

9.26. Compare and contrast the 13 problem-solving strategies presented in this chapter. Provide an example in which each might be used.

9.27. Four different kinds of analogies were suggested for use. Describe each and give an example when each would be useful.

9.28. How does each of the problem-solving problems relate to the anatomical parts of a problem? For example, irrelevant information causes people to consider solution paths that don't lead to the goal. How do the other problem-solving problems interfere with obtaining a direct route to the goal?

9.29. There are good and bad aspects to mechanization. What are they?

Return to the true–false questions you answered before you read chapter 9. Go over your responses and compare them with the correct answers. Answers 1. F 2. F 3. T 4. F 5. T 6. F 7. T 8. T 9. F 10. F

FIG. 9.3. Answer to Problem 9.7. This is a difficult problem because it requires that we break a mental set by rotating the horses 90° to a vertical position and by switching heads for each horse. (From M. Scheerer, Problem solving © 1963 by Scientific American, Inc. All rights reserved.)

Answer to 9.18: Ann Landers suggested that the exasperated husband surprise Louise with accordion lessons. She had no suggestions for what to do with Bernice and Murray.

10

CREATIVE THINKING

BEFORE YOU READ THE TENTH CHAPTER:
TRUE OR FALSE?

Circle the correct answer.

1. The creative process appears to be fundamentally different from the everyday thinking processes that most people use.

                T   F

2. Most great creative acts involve serendipity, a "happy accident" in which the creative individual is lucky enough to be at the right place at the right time.

                T   F

3. Thinking analogically requires the application of information that was learned in one context to a very different context.

                T   F

4. All of the strategies for enhancing creative thinking involve the "spread of activation" through the knowledge base that an individual has stored in memory.

                T   F

5. People who have many ideas are more likely to come up with good ideas than people who have few ideas.

                T   F

6. An environment that is supportive of the creative process is one in which individuals receive continuous rewards for their work.

                T   F

7. Because creative acts are, by definition, unusual, creative people tend to be less concerned about conformity than less creative people.

                T   F

8. Research has shown that it is not possible to increase creativity with training because the creative process does not follow rules.

                T   F

9. Creative people tend to be good at finding problems that most of us fail to recognize, in addition to being good problem solvers.

                T   F

10. The most important component of the creative process is a large, interconnected knowledge net.

                T   F

CHAPTER OBJECTIVES

The material presented in the chapter on creative thinking was designed to provide readers with an understanding of the creative process and with strategies that should increase the probability of a creative act. People are creative on a continuum, and virtually everyone has the ability to make creative contributions in various fields of knowledge. Creativity is not an either–or trait. Strategies that increase the flow of ideas and maximize the efficiency of the thinking process should increase creative thinking. The most important variables in encouraging critical thinking are a large, complex knowledge net and an attitude that supports an intimate involvement with the information. All of the strategies that are suggested to enhance creative thinking share the characteristic that they help people think in "new ways" about problems and situations.

Name: **Date:**   **Course/Section:**

Journal Entries

Record your thoughts as you reflect on the material in chapter 10. The purpose of this journal is to let you step back and reflect on the material that you are learning. It is a place to record your discussions with yourself. Write about topics that are unclear or seem particularly useful to you. This is the time to make your own connections between and within chapters, from class, and the real life that happens out of class. Use the next page for your second entry.

_____

Date of first entry

Name: **Date:**   **Course/Section:**

Journal—second entry for chapter 10:

_____

Date of second entry

Review of Skills for Creative Thinking

Category Description: These skills are all designed to help people increase the flow of ideas—a process that should increase the probability of a creative (i.e., novel and good) response.

Skill	Description	Examples of Use
Redefine the problem and goal	Phrase the problem in several different ways and come up with different types of solutions.	Instead of asking "How can I get a new job?" ask "What do I really want from a job?" or "How can I have more money?"
Find analogies	Apply solutions and ideas across different domains of knowledge.	Use knowledge about the ways animals keep cool to design a way to keep food cool.
List relevant terms	Before attempting a solution, write down all terms that come to mind when you think about the problem.	When thinking about ways to improve the possibilities for peace in the Middle East, list all the relevant terms that come to mind in a 10-minute interval.
Brainstorm	Without censoring or evaluation, list as many solutions to the problems as possible.	In finding ways to save money, list every money-saving idea you can. Best if done in a group.
Check lists	Generate and use lists of ways that a solution can vary.	If designing a new toy, list ways that toys can vary—size, color, etc.
List attributes	Create a matrix of relevant attributes and then combine cells.	List the parts of a dress and the ways each can differ, then create combinations.
Positive, negative, interesting	List the positive, negative, and interesting aspects of various solutions.	Use these three columns to evaluate solutions to the problem of world hunger.
Visualize	Image yourself as part of the problem and try to "see" it from other perspectives.	View the problem of teen violence from the perspective of the teens, police, victims, parents, etc.
Browse	Keep the problem in mind as you go about idea-enhancing activities.	Read, watch quality programs, write, etc., as you think about a problem.

ACTIVE LEARNING EXERCISES

Using the strategies for creative thinking presented in this chapter, give creative solutions to the following problems. Notice which of the creativity strategies you try for each problem and which one seems to work.

10.1. The 1958 Rockefeller Report on "The Pursuit of Excellence: Education and the Future of America" raised a number of still timely problems in need of creative solutions. Select one of the following problems. Restate the goal in at least four ways and then list some solutions that would "fit" each goal. Assume a different perspective, then list an additional goal and possible solutions for this goal.

A. How can we improve conditions for "giving free expression to creativity" within the realms of Science, Government, Business, and Education?

B. In what ways can colleges and universities provide the Best Climate for the Creativity of the Individual without sacrificing the Benefits of Group Organization?

C. How can we more quickly and surely identify the creative person and enhance his individuality?

10.2. Morale is low on the automobile assembly line. There is a heat wave that is affecting everybody's work, causing the employees to slow down and destroy the pace on the assembly line.

State the problem and the goal in three different ways.

List positives, negatives, and interesting aspects of each of the ways you defined the goal and each of the solutions you generated. Are you able to apply solutions from a different domain? What do teachers do on very hot days when they have to keep their students working? Are any of the strategies applicable to automobile assembly lines? Do any of your ideas meet the criteria for creativity?

10.3. An architectural firm has been given a difficult contract. They must build an essentially rectangular building to keep construction costs down, yet they want it to be aesthetic and match its colonial surroundings. What are some possible approaches? Visualize the possibilities. If possible, sketch some solutions. List the attributes for buildings and determine if you can use some combinations to create a novel and good design.

10.4. If you've ever had the distasteful experience of trying to get a young child to take unpleasant-tasting medicine, you'll know that this is a difficult task. How can you get a young child to take unpleasant-tasting medication? List two similar problems from different domains. Do they suggest a solution? Visualize this problem from the perspective of the child, the parent, the medicine, the spoon. Describe the process.

10.5. When college students move away from home and into the dorms, they often feel homesick. Because this seems like a childish problem, few will admit to it. What can be done to alleviate this problem? List other problems in which the people involved don't want to talk about the problem. Does this list suggest novel solutions? Redefine the problem in three different ways. Now list a solution to each redefinition of the problem.

10.6. Some young women literally starve themselves to death in order to gain the "super-thin" look that modern society endorses for women. What can we do about this problem?

Before answering this question, write down all of the relevant terms that come to mind as you think about the problem.

10.7. You have been commissioned to create stained-glass windows that depict the American Revolutionary War. What should you depict? How will you select your colors, etc.?

Visualize the possibilities. What sort of scene do you want to depict? Why? Imagine that you were a soldier in the American Revolution, a member of the English navy, the King of England, a Native American, etc. Do these different perspectives change what you want to depict?

10.8. Your boss just called and is on his way over for dinner. Using only the ingredients you have in your house, what would you make for dinner? Suppose each of the following: (a) your boss is a gourmet cook, (b) it is very hot in your house, (c) your boss is vegetarian, (d) you are on a low-calorie diet, (e) your spouse only eats rare meat and your boss finds rare meat disgusting, (f) your boss is kosher and you're not even sure what that means, and (g) you made pork and your boss is allergic to it. How do your plans change in each of these scenarios? How about having dinner delivered?

10.9. How would you design a costume to represent what the well-dressed young man or woman will wear in the year 2010?

Make a matrix of attributes. Browse through fashion magazines and costume books to increase the number and quality of your ideas.

10.10. The headquarters of a large corporation is faced with rising costs and declining profits. In order to remedy this problem they could:

A. Fire six employees.
B. Discontinue their new line of designer underwear.
C. Cheat on their taxes.
D. Require each employee to take a pay cut.
E. Ask each employee to work an extra hour each day.
F. Borrow money at high interest rates.

Evaluate the impact of each of these solutions and recommend additional ones.

10.11. Find a problem and suggest a solution. It can be something as silly as putting headlights on your cat's collar so she can be seen at night or as serious as designing a better cane for the blind.

10.12. Apply your problem-solving skills to a contemporary social issue such as eliminating racism, reducing pollution, or deescalating the arms race. You may use any of these suggestions or find a different contemporary problem. Go through the various strategies that are listed and see how the use of each one changes the nature of the problem and the response.

10.13. Read the biography of a famous creative person. How did he or she arrive at creative solutions? Can you discern anything notable in the individual's background or personality that can help to explain the nature of creativity? Is there evidence for intrinsic motivation?

10.14. Find poems and other forms of artistic expression that have used analogies. How does the analogy convey the meaning that is implied by the artist?

Exercise your creative abilities in some of the following:

10.15. Write captions for cartoons. As you do this, think about the use of the creative thinking strategies.

10.16. Doodle.

10.17. Integrate principles learned in one class into another entirely different subject area.

10.18. Keep an idea file. Jot down ideas as they come to you. Review them periodically and use them.

10.19. Think of ways to improve on a favorite toy—like a teddy bear.

10.20. Enjoy your creative thoughts.

THOUGHTFUL QUESTIONS

10.21. Why is creativity defined by its product and not the thinking process that went into the product?

10.22. Contrast the terms "vertical" and "lateral" thinking. Give an example of each. How is lateral thinking similar to redefining the problem?

10.23. What does it mean to say that it takes a prepared mind to recognize a serendipitous event?

10.24. Explain the idea of "release from fixation." How can this idea be used to explain insight and incubation?

10.25. What is the relationship between intelligence and creativity?

10.26. What kind of environment will foster creativity? How can intrinsic motivation be promoted in the classroom and the workplace?

10.27. Explain why the formation of analogies is often considered an essential step in the process of creativity.

10.28. Why is it important to defer judgment during brainstorming?

10.29. How are creative ideas checklists used? Compare them with the strategy of attribute listing.

10.30. What is the principle behind plus, minus, interesting?

10.31. Describe the program in which children had to list topic-relevant words before writing. What was the effect on the outcome? Why?

10.32. Design a learning environment that would foster creative thinking.

10.33. Why should we try to "make the familiar strange?"

Return to the true–false questions you answered before you read chapter 10. Look over your responses and compare them with the correct answers. Answers: 1. F 2. F 3. T 4. T 5. T 6. F 7. T 8. F 9. T 10. T

11

THE LAST WORD

This is the last chapter in the book. The corresponding text chapter is just one short page that explains the need to put thinking skills together because they cannot be separated meaningfully when we are thinking in the real world and asks you to "step back" and reflect on the material presented. Problems do not come neatly labeled as hypothesis testing or reasoning or likelihood and uncertainty. For this reason, the active learning problems that are presented in this chapter require the reader to use combinations of skills. I provide some hints to keep you on the right track. I hope that you enjoy working on these problems and that you feel that you are becoming a better thinker because of your experiences with this book.

SELF-RATING OF CRITICAL THINKING SKILLS AND DISPOSITIONS

Evaluate Your Thinking Skills and Dispositions

In the introductory chapter, you rated your own thinking and made judgments about your strengths and weaknesses. Without looking back at your answers, reconsider your strengths and weaknesses now that you have read the accompanying text and worked your way through the exercises in this book. Consider each of the thinking skills listed next. Rate your ability with each of the skills using the following scale:

1   2   3   4   5   6   7   8   9   10
extremely poor   average   superior

___ 1. *Recognition, identification and control of variables*—Recognizing, controlling, or weighing multiple influences in solving problems. For example, interpreting historical phenomena by sorting political and social factors using the available information and deciding whether there are cause and effect relationships or whether variables are too confounded to permit a reliable inference.

___ 2. *Awareness of gaps in knowledge or information*—Recognizing when you have failed to understand material because you can't establish the meaning of a term or there is incomplete information provided.

___ 3. *Understanding the need for operational definitions*—Recognizing when a concept has not been clearly defined and the need for using only words of prior definition in forming a new definition.

___ 4. *Considering the strength of the reasons that support a conclusion*—Listing the reasons in an argument and considering how well they support a conclusion along with assumptions, qualifiers, and counterarguments that impact on the level of support.

___ 5. *Drawing inferences from data and evidence, including correlational reasoning*—Considering sample size, measurement, and convergent validity when assessing empirical data.

___ 6. *Using rational criteria when making decisions*—Listing and weighing alternatives and criteria that are important in reaching a decision.

___ 7. *Systematically applying a plan for solving problems*—Being consciously aware of problem-solving strategies and applying them systematically when faced with a difficult decision.

___ 8. *Reading for comprehension*—Monitoring comprehension of difficult text and knowing when to reread and when to skim; includes the frequent use of paraphrase and summaries.

___ 9. *Concern for accuracy*—Habitually checking work for accuracy and for comprehension.

___ 10. *Trying creative approaches*—Making the effort to generate novel and useful responses to problems.

___ 11. *Deliberately using multiple modes of thought*—Trying to think in spatial, verbal, and nonverbal modes.

___ 12. *Working in a planful manner*—Looking ahead and anticipating difficulties when working on a problem.

___ 13. *Communication skills*—Communicating clearly and effectively when speaking and writing.

___ 14. *Recognizing propaganda*—Recognizing propagandistic techniques that are designed as emotional appeals.

___ 15. *Maintaining an open attitude*—Willingness to suspend judgment and to accept a nonpreferred alternative if it is well reasoned.

Look back over your answers. Do you see any patterns of weaknesses or strengths? Compare the way you answered these questions today with the way you answered them before you read the text and worked through the exercises. I expect that you rated yourself *lower* on some of the skills than you did at the start of the book, probably because you are now more aware of what these skills entail. A lower self-rating does not mean that you lost ability; more likely it means that you are better able to make thoughtful judgments.

ACTIVE LEARNING EXERCISES

Use the critical thinking skills that you developed in this book to answer the following:

11.1. Suppose that you are serving on a jury and you are hearing evidence about the guilt or innocence of a robbery suspect. To determine if she is guilty, a sample of her hair is compared to hair found at the scene of the crime. The two hair samples match. Would you consider the suspect more likely to be the robber if the hair at the scene of the crime is indistinguishable from the hair of 1% of the population than if it were indistinguishable from 20% of the population? (This problem is adapted from Arkes, 1989.) Why did you answer the way you did? How would you explain your answer to other members of the jury who say that this doesn't matter because we cannot be 100% certain in either case?

11.2. The following statement is taken from campaign material that was mailed to my home from the Democratic National Committee (entitled, "Let's Look at the Record," received in November 1994): "Do we want to empower Americans to compete and win or support the power grab of the GOP Congressional leadership?"

Explain the sorts of persuasive techniques that are being used in this question. Can you identify the fallacy that is being committed? If so, what is it?

11.3. Suppose that you are deciding if a new television show is funny. Zimbardo and Leippe (1991) cited evidence that people rate shows as funnier when laugh tracks are used on the shows than when they aren't. Explain how this would influence your judgments about how funny a show is.

11.4. You are interested in determining if a weight-loss club really helps people lose weight. The club advertises that out of 138 people who started the program 1 year ago, 81 are still attending and they lost an average of 14.7 pounds. What additional information would you want to know? What can you conclude (Lehman & Nisbett, 1993)?

11.5. A commonly heard argument that appears in pro-Communist publications goes something like this: Under Communism, Russia had virtually no crime. Now that it is becoming capitalist, crime is soaring. It is clear that the change to capitalism has caused the crime. Comment on this causal statement.

11.6. Yu-chin is an attractive, well-dressed woman with carefully polished nails and well-done hair. Which of the following is most likely to be true about Yu-chin? Why did you select the answer that you did?

> She is most probably a salesperson.
> She is most probably a model.
> She is most probably a physicist.
> This is a stupid question because we cannot make any probability statements.

11.7. According to Liebman (1992), Lender's Bagels say Blueberry, but they contain more dried colored apple pieces than blueberries in them. (The apple pieces are colored blue, of course.) The picture on Lean Cuisine Glazed Chicken with Vegetable Rice shows six thick slices of mushrooms, yet on analysis, it contains about ⅓ of a mushroom. What are the strategies behind these labeling and picture "gimmicks." How can they be used to persuade us to buy products that are not what they seem?

11.8. If you are a highly talented squash player who is playing against a less talented novice, should you choose a 5-point or 1-point tie breaker? Why (adapted from Fong, Krantz, & Nisbett, 1986)?

11.9. Suppose that you want to learn about attitudes toward some controversial subject such as whether retarded adults should be allowed to care for their own children. How would you design a good study that would provide a valid index of what people in North America think about this topic?

11.10. The following is taken verbatim from a page-long advertisement ("We Are Fed Up") that appeared in many national newspapers in the United States on June 1, 1993. It was written to persuade readers that they should fight the decision by the ABC television network to air an R-rated series:

Dr. Branden S. Centerwall, an epidemiologist at the University of Washington, in a recent study showed that the white homicide rate in the U.S. **increased** 93% between the introduction of TV in 1945 and 1974; in Canada 92%. In South Africa, which had no TV until 1974, it declined 7% during the same time period.

Comment on this information. Does it support the idea that television has caused violence to increase? Why do you think that the authors of this advertisement specify "white homicide rate?"

11.11. In a paper that was written about needle exchange programs, I read the following: "To not implement a needle exchange program is to condone genocide." How would you respond to this statement, regardless of your views on needle exchange programs?

11.12. This is almost too silly to write about without laughing, but it is a true story. A doctor appeared on a daytime talk show claiming that he could hypnotize women so that they could enlarge their bust size. As evidence of his success, he brought along several women who offered testimonials that his techniques worked. As an amiable skeptic, respond to this approach. Can you conclude that it worked for some people based on the testimonials?

11.13. A student once asked if it were possible to remember one's own birth. How would you design an experiment that would answer this question?

11.14. Many people believe that premenstrual syndrome (PMS) is common among women, yet the research data show that it is very rare. Almost 50% of the women who report that they have PMS actually show no relationship between their symptoms and their menstrual cycles (Wade, 1995). Why does this belief persist when research shows that it is really very unusual?

11.15. David, an avid sports fan, found a unique way of getting a clearer picture on his TV to watch the Grey Cup game. In telling a friend about this incident, David points out that:

- He kicked the TV to get a clearer picture of the curling and hockey match.
- The vertical and horizontal hold on the TV was stable after he kicked it.

- David watches TV sports in the living room and sits on the couch.
- He had a poor picture of the Grey Cup game until he kicked the TV. (Amsel, Langer, & Loutzenhiser, 1991, p. 239)

If you wanted to convince someone that kicking the TV caused a better picture, rate each of the preceding statements on how relevant it is to establishing cause using 1 = not at all relevant and 5 = very highly relevant. Why did you select the ratings that you chose?

11.16. The following excerpt is taken verbatim from an advertisement ("Psych Yourself Up") for a phone-in psychic. (It appeared in *Cosmopolitan* magazine, January 1994.)

Scientific Proof: A good psychic reading will usually astound newcomers to this arena. But those who are familiar with the field know that psychic power has been tested and authenticated by some very prestigious and scientific organizations, including some of the nation's top ten universities. Psychic investigations are even being conducted by our national military and intelligence agencies which have actually used psychics to spy on enemy weaponry.

How good is this "scientific proof?" Comment on the claims that are being made to support the conclusion that psychics are able to know the future.

11.17. Suppose that you learn that a certain food is statistically associated with some disease. Researchers found twice the rate of the disease in people who ate the food compared to those who didn't eat the food. Suppose further that both groups had 10,000 subjects in them. The group that ate the food had six cases of the disease and the group that didn't eat the food had three cases of the disease. What can you conclude (adapted from Dawes, 1994)?

11.18. I received an exciting letter in the mail from the "World of Wealth." The letter informed me of my great luck in being selected to enter a contest. This part is verbatim: "Diane, respond with fee, complete all steps" and "if you win first prize, it will be official. I would make the following announcement—pending approval—DIANE HALPERN IS THE $10,000.00 CASH WINNER!"

Well, what do you think? Should I spend the money to enter this contest? Why did they use my name in virtually every line in this letter? Why did they tell me that "taxes would not be prepaid?" In the very fine print on the back, they add that 1,570,500 total entries are expected. Should this number influence whether or not I spend my money to play this contest?

11.19. Homelessness is a major problem in the United States and many other places in the world. State the goal for this ill-defined problem in four different ways and list some possible solutions to the problem of homelessness that are suggested by the way you stated the goal. Given what you just learned from this exercise, what would you suggest as a way to reduce the problem of homelessness?

11.20. Find a news story or an advertisement that relies on statistics. Explain if the statistics are being used correctly or incorrectly.

11.21. Read through the "letter to the editor" section of your local newspaper. Comment on the reasoning that is used in three different letters. How well are the conclusions supported? Can you spot any errors?

11.22. Suppose you want to buy your dream car and you've narrowed your search down to three models. Using the decision-making worksheet that follows, answer the following questions.

Problem: Which car to buy?

Considerations	Honda	Chevrolet	Yugo
Price (5)	-2	+1	+2
Miles per gallon (4)	+1	0	-1
Appearance (3)	+2	+1	-1

(a) Do the necessary computations from the preceding worksheet to decide which car to buy using the overall assessment method. Which car should you select?

(b) Do the necessary computation to decide which car to buy using the dimensional comparison method. Based on this method, which car should you select?

(c) Do the necessary computations to decide which car to buy using the $\frac{2}{3}$ ideal rule. According to this method, your dream car should have a minimum score of ____?
Based on this method, which car should you buy?

11.23. Suppose you believe that:

All Democrats are tax and spend liberals.
Candidate X is a tax and spend liberal.

Is it valid to conclude that Candidate X is a Democrat? Show your work.

11.24. Select a photograph from a recent newspaper or news magazine. What does it show you? Describe it in words, and then compare your words with the photo. Is the photo more memorable or more likely to sway opinion? Why? What sorts of visual devices are used in the photo? Is there an expression on the face of a person that would be difficult to convey in words? What is at the center of the photo? What activity and mood are depicted?

11.25. Here is a summary of a California state proposition that appeared in *The Los Angeles Times* on October 25, 1992, p. T4.

Proposition 163—Snack Tax:

What it is:

This proposition would repeal the sales tax on snack food, candy and bottled water enacted by the Legislature and Gov. Pete Wilson in 1991 to help cover a projected $14 billion shortfall. The measure would reduce state tax revenues by about $330 million annually, while cities and counties would lose about $120 million a year. This is a proposed law and constitutional amendment placed on the ballot by petition.

Arguments for:

Proponents say the tax on snacks, candy and bottled water amounts to a tax on the essentials of life. They say the sales tax is the most regressive tax because the poor use a proportionately higher share of their income for purchases and therefore bear a greater burden of the tax relative to their ability to pay.

Arguments against:

There is no formal opposition to this measure, but the arguments made for the tax when it was enacted was that the state needed more revenue.

Using this information, identify reasons for and against the proposition. Rate them for their strength. Add any relevant information that might be missing. List additional information that you would like to have before voting. How would you vote on this proposition?

11.26. Write a letter to me (the author of your text) explaining what was useful about the text and what needs to be improved. If you have suggestions or good examples for the next edition, please let me know. If I use your suggestion, I will be certain to reference your letter. You can write to me at: Dr. Diane F. Halpern, Department of Psychology, California State University, San Bernardino, 5500 University Parkway, San Bernardino, CA 92407 USA.

REFERENCES

Amsel, E., Langer, R., & Loutzenhiser, L. (1991). Do lawyers reason differently from psychologists? A comparative design for studying expertise. In R. J. Sternberg & P. A. Frensch (Eds.), *Complex problem solving: Principles and mechanisms* (pp. 223–250). Hillsdale, NJ: Lawrence Erlbaum Associates.

Arkes, H. (1989). Principles in judgement/decision making research pertinent to legal proceedings. *Behavioral Sciences and the Law, 7*(4), 429–456.

Atkinson, R. C. (1975). Mnemotechnics in second-language learning. *American Psychologist, 30,* 821–828.

Bennett, W. (1990, March). Should drugs be legalized? *Reader's Digest,* p. 90.

Bereiter, C. (1984). How to keep thinking skills from going the way of all frills. *Educational Leadership, 42,* 75–77.

Black, H., & Black, S. (1985). *Book-3 Verbal building thinking skills.* Pacific Grove, CA: Midwest Publications.

British Broadcasting Company. (1994, April 2). Radio News.

Cheng, P. W., Holyoak, K. J., Nisbett, R. E., & Oliver, L. M. (1986). Pragmatic versus syntactic approaches to training deductive reasoning. *Cognitive Psychology, 18,* 293–328.

Cialdini, R. B. (1993). *Influence: Science and practice* (3rd ed.). Glenview, IL: Scott, Foresman.

Dawes, R. M. (1979). The robust beauty of improper linear models in decision making. *American Psychologist, 34,* 571–582.

Dawes, R. M. (1994). *House of cards: Psychology and psychotherapy built on myth.* New York: The Free Press.

Democratic National Committee. (1994, November). *Let's look at the record.*

Einhorn, H. J., & Hogarth, R. M. (1978). Confidence in judgement: Persistence of the illusion of validity. *Psychological Review, 85,* 395–416.

Fong, G. T., Krantz, D. H., & Nisbett, R. E. (1986). The effects of statistical training on thinking about everyday problems. *Cognitive Psychology, 18,* 253–292.

Galotti, K. M. (1995). Reasoning about reasoning: A course project. In D. F. Halpern & S. G. Nummedal (Eds.), Psychologists teach critical thinking [Special issue]. *Teaching of Psychology, 22,* 66–68.

Gardner, M. (1978). *Aha! Insight.* New York: Freeman.

Henle, M. (1962). On the relation between logic and thinking. *Psychological Review, 69,* 366–378.

Landers, A. (1992, January 1). Wife's music finally has hit a sour note. *The Los Angeles Times.*

Lehman, D. R., & Nisbett, R. E. (1993). A longitudinal study of the effects of undergraduate training on reasoning. In R. E. Nisbett (Ed.), *Rules for reasoning* (pp. 340–357). Hillsdale, NJ: Lawrence Erlbaum Associates.

Liebman, B. (1992, March). The name game: Let them eat buzzwords. *Nutrition Action Healthletter,* p. 8.

Loftus, E. F. (1980). *Memory: Surprising new insights into how we remember and why we forget.* Reading, MA: Addison-Wesley.

Lubell, A. (1989, November). Chronic brain injuries in boxers: Is it avoidable? *The Physician and Sports Medicine,* pp. 126–131.

Mac Kenzie, J. (1994, February 9). Magazine's publisher jailed for pornography. *The Moscow Times,* p. 2.

McGovern, T. V., & Hogshead, D. L. (1990). Learning about writing, thinking about thinking [Special Issue]. Psychologists teach writing. *Teaching of Psychology, 17*, 5–10.

Meyers, C., & Jones, T. B. (1993). *Promoting active learning: Strategies for the college classroom.* San Francisco: Jossey-Bass.

Miller, R. H., Kupsh, J., & Larson Jones, C. (1994). Software ethics: Teaching by example. In D. F. Halpern (Ed.), *Changing college classrooms: New teaching and learning strategies for an increasingly complex world* (pp. 254–267). San Francisco: Jossey-Bass.

Newell, A., & Simon, H. A. (1972). *Human problem solving.* Englewood Cliffs, NJ: Prentice-Hall.

Pickren, J. W., & Gamarra, M. C. (1975). Effects of smoking. In G. P. Murphy, D. Pressman, & E. A. Mirand (Eds.), *Perspectives in cancer research and treatment.* New York: Liss.

Psych yourself up. (1994, January). *Cosmopolitan Magazine.*

Reed, S. K. (1982). *Cognition: Theory and applications.* Monterey, CA: Brooks/Cole.

Rosenthal, R., & Jacobson, L. (1968). *Pygmalion in the classroom. Teacher expectations and pupils' intellectual development.* New York: Holt.

Rubinstein, M. F., & Pfeiffer, K. R. (1980). *Concepts in problem solving.* Englewood Cliffs, NJ: Prentice-Hall.

Scheerer, M. (1963). Problem solving. *Scientific American, 208*, 118–128.

Seech, Z. (1993). *Open minds and everyday reasoning.* Belmont, CA: Wadsworth.

Should the Catholic Church throw out its rule on celibacy for priests and nuns. (1994, June 21). *San Francisco Chronicle*, p. A19.

Wade, C. (1995). Using writing to develop and assess critical thinking. In D. F. Halpern & S. G. Nummedal (Eds.), Psychologists teach critical thinking p-[Special issue]. *Teaching of Psychology, 22*, 24–28.

Wason, P. C. (1969). Structure simplicity and psychological complexity. *Bulletin of the British Psychological Society, 22*, 281–284.

We are fed up! (1993, June 1). *Los Angeles Times*, p. H/8.

Wickelgren, W. (1974). *How to solve problems.* San Francisco: Freeman.

Zimbardo, P. G., & Leippe, M. R. (1991). *The psychology of attitude change and social influence.* New York: McGraw-Hill.